Sales Integration

The 4th Wave of Sales

Dennis Galbraith

Contact:
Dennis Galbraith Enterprises
DennisGalbraith@msn.com

Blog postings and interactive examples related to Sales Integration are available at RevenueGuru.com

ISBN: 1-453-74982-9

For my sons, may they too benefit from the freedom they provide.

SSG Kristopher Renno, U.S. Army's 82nd Airborne Division at Fort Bragg, NC

SSG Marc Renno, U.S. Army's 797th EOD Unit at Fort Hood, TX

Cadet Travis Galbraith, U.S. Army ROTC at Texas Christian University

Contents

Introduction

Sales Integration – Facilitating each individual shopper's sales process across all interactive touchpoints

Business runs on sales. The world is embarking on an entirely new wave in selling, replacing the old notion of a salesperson exclusively handing the sales process. The internet is often viewed as another form of media, comparable to TV, radio, and newspaper. This is far from the case. The internet has ears. Interactivity means the ability to listen and respond. That one attribute is responsible for this new wave in selling. Selling is an interactive process, and those sales interactions often begin online. Successful participation in this new world requires a new way of looking at how products are sold: a shopper's perspective. When individuals grasp the holistic understanding of the new sales process, even those who previously did not recognize they were involved in sales find there has never been a more exciting time to be in the profession.

The salesperson's control of the sales process is legendary and, in many cases, infamous. Children's fables warn of salespeople the way they warn of monsters. A salesperson tricks Jack into buying magical beans. The wicked witch disguises herself as a salesperson to trick Sleeping Beauty into biting the poison apple. Salespeople con the emperor into parading down the street with no clothes on. From the time children are taught about money, and often before, most are taught not to trust salespeople.

Today, consumers enjoy transparency into the market and control in defining their own sales process. They bounce across distribution channels in shopping paths no marketer ever designed. We now live in an exciting world where shoppers spontaneously create their own sales processes. Shoppers changed the world by individually and independently acting in their own best interest. I did not invent sales integration. I simply recognized the need for it while working with mounds of consumer research data.

As I helped hundreds of businesses respond to this sweeping change, I began to understand its depth and breadth. The purpose of this book is to help business leaders and those involved in facilitating the sales process to understand what has happened to their world and how to adapt to it faster.

Multichannel Marketing, Multiple-Channel Marketing, and Sales Integration

The first time I taught students about multichannel marketing I was using the seventh edition of Philip Kotler's textbook, *Marketing Management*, published in 1991. At that time, multichannel marketing meant offering goods or services to different segments through different distribution channels.

As an example, the text used IBM's introduction to personal computers. It began selling through Sears, Computerland, and other stores. IBM also sold its PCs through value-added resellers and its own sales force.

Over the years, the meaning of the term multichannel marketing changed. In a 2005 article in *Journal of Interactive Marketing*[1], Arvind Rangaswamy and Gerrit H. Van Bruggen explained the changing definition of the term multichannel marketing:

> It is becoming common for customers to use different channels at different stages of their decision-and-shopping cycles, for example, using Web sites to obtain information but making purchases offline; in the past they typically obtained all their channel services from a single integrated channel at all stages of their decision process. We refer to customers who use more than one channel to interact with firms as multichannel customers, and marketing strategies to reach such customers as multichannel marketing.

They went on later in the article to differentiate multichannel marketing from multiple-channel marketing.

> It is important to recognize that multichannel marketing is not the same as traditional multiple-channel marketing, in which a firm interacts with different segments of the customer base through different channels.

I am proud to say this article referenced my research at J.D. Power and Associates. More importantly, there was recognition of fact that the consumer was taking over. Note that in Kotler's 1991 text, that definition of multichannel marketing was a choice made by business. Sometimes this choice was in response to competitors and sometimes it was to gain competitive advantage, but the shoppers had no say in the matter. In Rangaswamy and Van Bruggen's definition, multichannel marketing is something businesses must work at in response to multichannel shopping.

Wikipedia references the article by Rangaswamy and Van Bruggen in its brief article for multichannel marketing:

> Multichannel marketing is marketing using many different marketing channels to reach a customer. In this sense, a channel might be a retail store, a web site, a mail order catalogue, or direct personal communications by letter, email, or text

---

[1]"Opportunities and Challenges in Multichannel Marketing: An Introduction to the Special Issue," Arvind Rangaswamy and Gerrit H. Van Bruggen, *Journal of Interactive Marketing*; Spring 2005.

message. The objective of the company doing the marketing is to make it easy for a consumer to buy from them in whatever way is most appropriate. To be effective multichannel marketing needs to be supported by good supply chain management systems, so that the details and prices of goods on offer are consistent across the different channels. It might also be supported by detailed analysis of the return on investment from each different channel, measured in terms of customer response and conversion of sales. Some companies target certain channels at different demographic segments of the market at different socio-economic groups of consumers.

This definition resembles a blend between Rangaswamy and Van Bruggen and the old textbook definition. What is most bothersome to me is the term "to reach a customer." Multichannel marketing uses many different marketing channels to sell to a customer. Recognizing each interactive touchpoint in a multichannel marketing network as a sales function is the heart of sales integration. The following story pulls all these definitions together:

Chad sold healthy oatmeal treats through his store, through his website (ChadsOatmealTreats.com), and through a website offering healthy treats from multiple companies (HealthyTreats4You.com). Chad was practicing multiple-channel marketing. A shopper could buy his products from any of these three channels.

It came to Chad's attention that shoppers were bouncing around across these channels, as well as other websites, as they shopped for healthy snacks. One shopper behaved like this

> HealthyTreats4You.com
> to ChadsOatmealTreats.com
> to a search engine
> to BestOats.com (makers of the brand of oats Chad uses exclusively)
> back to ChadsOatmealTreats.com
> to Chad's store, where the purchase was made.

Chad recognized his customers where practicing multichannel shopping.

In response, Chad made it possible to open the manufacturer's site, BestOats.com, from ChadsOatmealTreats.com. He made sure shoppers on ChadsOatmealTreats.com could not only order online but also contact the store by phone, email, or chat. He put a map and directions to his store on ChadsOatmealTreats.com as well. Chat worked out a deal with Best Oats to provide information about his products on their website, complete with a link to his website and contact information to his store. By facilitating the multichannel shopping of his customers, Chad was practicing multichannel marketing in its most modern definition.

After reading this book, Chad scanned the many interactive touchpoints to make sure he was doing everything possible to sell his products. He recognized none of the touchpoints described above were interruption advertising. Shoppers went there because they wanted to; they were interested in buying, and they were in control of the sales process. Chad provided tools on his website and on HealthyTreats4You.com making it easy for the shopper to match his products to their tastes, occasions, and serving requirements. He even put a computer in his store. It was open to his website, so those waiting for service could match themselves up with the right products. He made sure the benefits of his products were demonstrated. He made changes to his online shopping cart to make it easier to purchase. Alternately, shoppers could abandon the shopping cart and order over the phone. His sales people knew the information on his website, and had the site open in front of them as they answered the phone.

Chad examined his product delivery from all sales channels to make sure the product was consistently presented in the most appealing way possible. He set up an opt-in system reminding customers to check their weight and blood pressure and to reorder more of his snacks. He approached multichannel marketing with the recognition the shopper was in control of the sales process. He responded to his shoppers' needs by not only facilitating their travel from site to site but facilitating their sales process across all interactive touchpoints on all related sites. Everyone on Chad's team was working together to facilitate a nearly infinite number of sales processes in a way that enhanced quality of life for the shoppers, employees, owners, and the community. They were practicing sales integration.

Sales vs. Marketing

One might argue the world would be a better place if sales departments had taken responsibility for websites rather than marketing and IT. Gerhard Gschwandtner, Publisher and Founder of Selling Power Magazine, describes the difference between the way marketing and sales approach a customer as much like the difference between a composer writing a symphony and a jazz artist. Marketing evokes predictable emotions while sales is the art of the moment. Great sales people are agile and responsive.

In a classical sense, sales is part of marketing (product, price, promotions, and distribution). However, many marketing departments have an advertising orientation. Communications are primarily a one-way street from the company to the consumer. But the internet has ears. It listens to shoppers and responds, then it listens some more.

No one knows what the shopper will do, and each shopper is unique. Multichannel marketing requires integration across marketing and sales departments in a way that both sells and recognizes the shopper's control of the sales process. Designing a website that sells requires thinking like a salesperson. The site must be nimble and ready for a variety of shopping paths. Working across a plethora of websites, stores, catalogs, and direct marketing is the ultimate sales job. Sales people are not used to shoppers being in control and marketers are not used to back and forth interaction with customers. Each has a great deal to learn from the other if success is to be achieved. This book ends with a tool to facilitate the collaboration between sales and marketing departments.

Shopping Process and Sales Process

Some will complain I have not differentiated between shopping and selling. For many, shopping is what the buyer does and selling is what the seller does. It is hard to reconcile this old point of view with a consumer-centric approach to sales. Even prior to the internet, one could have asked, "Shouldn't the sales process match the shopping process?" Indeed, modern CRM systems for B-to-B selling capture the customers buying process.

The revolutionary change is the degree to which the shopper is in charge. Online there is no eye contact, no social pressure, no embarrassment, and no feelings of guilt or intimidation. Sellers provide online tools and information but have no control over how they are used or if they are used. Many sales professionals rely on a great deal of influence, yet the sales process is starting online, in an environment where they have little influence and no control. To recognize that the sales process starts online is to recognize that the shopper controls a huge portion of the sales process.

Whether one calls it a sales process or a shopping process, the bottom line is the shopper is in control to a degree unimaginable to previous generations. The shopper's ability to see the market at a glance, move about it at will, and go beyond the retailer for product knowledge and advice is revolutionary. If responded to properly, the results will be a more efficient economy, a broadening of sales skills across more jobs than ever, and more respect for the profession of selling.

I prefer the term sales process because it places the responsibility on business to live up to the demands of the process. We are not passive victims of a new age. Businesses have an opportunity to meet the needs of shoppers better than ever before.

The Immeasurable Contribution of Sales

The satisfaction a society receives in a year is not covered by common economic statistics. How much was produced and sold is one thing. Whether or not it was sold to the right people for the right purpose and whether those products were delivered in a way that maximized satisfaction is yet another. Whether or not those buyers purchase again delivers a huge impact on future economic growth. How sales professionals carry out the sales process remains largely ignored in economics.

Fortunately, whether or not an economist measures something does not make that thing any less real or less important. Sales are the driving force of business; there is no getting around that. When done right, a great sales experience sends consumers back to work eager to earn more and spend more in a marketplace promising enhanced quality of life. Done poorly, sales can breed the kind of distrust hindering economic growth and prosperity.

People cannot achieve nearly the quality of life in isolation that they can when they exchange goods, services, and labor in a free market place. Dialing that up to its maximum capability requires the best sales processes possible. For those of us passionate about sales and customer satisfaction, this is our age.

This book is critical, and much of that criticism is aimed at very fine organizations. An optimist sees fault in the current state relative to what can be. If current operations are sufficient, there is nothing more to be optimistic about.

Shortcomings of This Book

This book is not comprehensive on the subject of sales integration. No one person is capable of that. For example, shopping on television (e.g. HSN) is something I know very little about and have not covered sufficiently. This book is intended as a starting point to be built upon for many years to come.

Nearly all the examples in this book involved business-to-consumer (B-to-C) marketing. I've been involved in business-to-business (B-to-B) sales enough to know many of the same concepts apply, but more work is necessary in this area.

Most of the examples are from North America. My modest passport does not include enough business experience in any other market to consider myself an expert. In countries where trade is free and the internet provides market transparency, the concept of sales integration should apply without need of modification. In markets without this freedom and openness, some of the lessons of this book may not apply.

I relied heavily on examples from the auto industry, because that is where I started this work and know it best. I have worked in enough other industries to be certain the concept is universal. Nonetheless, other industries will be better served over time as examples and training more specific to them are developed.

Preview

The book is broken into four parts:
       Part One, The Concept of Sales Integration
       Part Two, The Sales Process
       Part Three, Vertical and Horizontal Sales Integration
       Part Four, Moving Forward

In Part One, the origins of sales integration are addressed, including a brief history of sales leading up to this point. In my research, the landscape we operate in today became much clearer for me after studying where we have been. I take some liberty in describing sales integration as the fourth wave of sales. I found nothing depicting sales history as a series of waves, and I am more a student than a scholar on the history of sales. Nonetheless, understanding sales history within some framework aids the reader's ability to understand where we are now, why things changed, and why adaptation is necessary.

The most important realization of my sales and marketing career was the day I recognized the Internet has ears. Combining this fact with the multichannel shopping I saw in my research led to the basic concept of sales integration. The advent of interactive software provided the inflection point leading to the fourth wave of sales.

Part Two covers the sales process, which never changed. While the process of selling has been described in many ways, the best I found is listening, matchmaking, demonstrating, closing, delivering, and managing the account. This book can easily be adapted to any reasonable definition of the sales process extending from the initial interaction to the post-close interactions leading to loyalty and advocacy.

Part Three is a ride through the shopper's many points of interaction through the sales process. Not all points apply to all industries, and new points will continue to rise. The shopper controls the sales process, which is often unique and non-linear.

In Part Four, we explore the difficult issues of price and value demonstration. The concept of value parity is introduced, followed by a discussion about the importance of demonstrating the value added by retailers. A story set in the year 2022 brings to life sales integration and the positive benefits it brings. To better make the vision a reality, the Mouse Chart is introduced as a method of facilitating the complex task of the new sales management.

Part 1

The Sales Integration Concept

Chapter 1

The Fourth Wave of Sales

The concept of sales integration is best presented in a historical context. Sales integration is the fourth large wave of sales:

1. Market Sales – Push within the distribution channel. Buyers and sellers come together at the market place.(e.g. flea market or farmers' market)
2. Peddler Sales – Push the distribution channel. Sellers bring the product to the buyers (e.g. traveling salesman, door-to-door sales, direct mail, and telemarketing)
3. Advertising to Sales – Interruption advertising pushes customers to the distribution channel. This is often seen in franchise systems, durable goods sales, and branded consumer packaged goods.
4. Sales Integration – Consumer takes control of the sales process. Companies facilitate the sales process across all interactive touchpoints.

The following series of stories – one for each wave of sales – lays a background for where sales efforts have been and where they must proceed. Examples from each wave will continue to live on, but sales integration will be the dominant model for the foreseeable future.

Market Sales (a story taking place many centuries ago)

Months ago, Greta learned to trust Gar, who makes furniture from wood. When they first met, he took the time to show her what a quality chair looked like. He even showed her what characteristics to avoid and why. Free to take this newfound knowledge anywhere in the market, she shopped around. She looked at the chairs of other vendors and returned to Gar. The products of some vendors were clearly inferior. Some vendors made chairs that appeared to be as good as Gar's, but those vendors did not add value by offering information to make her a better shopper. Surely, if their products were the best, they would have wanted her to know as much as possible about how to assess those products. Greta bought her chair from Gar back then and continues to view the transaction favorably.

Today, Greta enters the village market with currency and goods with which to trade. As she walks through the market, venders bark at her to examine their products and allow them to examine hers. She dealt with some of the vendors before. Some, like Gar, can be trusted, others cannot. It is late in the spring, and she needs a hog she can fatten up to provide food through the winter.

Until last year, this was the work of her father and brother, but both passed away. Now she must obtain the knowledge they were unable to pass on to her. She seeks Gar's advice on the swine.

Gar knows a little about hogs, but what he knows he learned from Jacob. Jacob is the most knowledgeable hog trader, so Gar refers Greta to Jacob.

Jacob knows that other vendors offer hogs of equal quality at a fair price. They also offer sickly hogs at the same price. Jacob knows some vendors will say whatever they think they need to in order to win Greta's confidence in them.

Jacob takes a different approach. He helps Greta become confident in herself. Like many shoppers, Greta is skeptical of all merchants to some degree. If Jacob wins her confidence, he may be able to charge Greta more than the market rate. However, the relationship will last only as long as his decisions for her are worth more than his premium, or until some other vendor says something to tarnish his image.

Jacob believes he will earn more money over the long run by selling at the market rate to a confident and informed customer. There are many days when he questions this belief. It often seems as though the rewards of his candor do not match the riches massed by the swindlers. It takes a lot of fair and honest deals to equal the gain that comes from selling a sick and worthless hog to an unsuspecting shopper.

Greta is a shrewd negotiator. She knows she cannot get ahead by paying more for products than others do. Even if she could survive a poor transaction, her pride would be hurt upon finding out she made one. Greta is, above all else, a proud buyer. In her view, exchange only takes place in order to enhance quality of life. After leaving her fields walking miles to the market, the exchange will be worth it or it will not be repeated.

Long before the term BATNA would ever be coined, Greta learns she must know what her alternatives are, her Best Alternative to a Negotiated Agreement. Extracting this information is difficult. She goes from one vendor to another, entering into tough negotiations before identifying what she believes is that vendor's best offer. Comparing offers is difficult when one must work to identify the real offer price.

Greta returns to Jacob and expresses appreciation for his helpful information; however, she is a poor farmer and cannot afford to pay even a small premium for her hog. She tells Jacob about the offer she believes is superior and offers Jacob a chance to match that offer. Jacob points out that getting the hog home will be difficult for someone unaccustomed to handling it. He will take Greta and the hog back in his wagon. He will also stop by each week for a month to see how the hog is doing.

The beauty of Greta's raven-black hair may play a role in Jacob's offer. Nevertheless, he knows selling does not stop at the close. Great delivery and account management are what bring customers back. If all goes well with this hog, Jacob will have a beautiful new customer for years to come.

This first wave of sales remains evident in modern shopping malls. Shoppers still go to market seeking advice. However, the expertise in physical stores selling merchandise has never been lower. Retail outlets often staff themselves with clerks more adept at keeping shelves stocked than moving merchandise off of them. The greater focus today is on turning retail stores into better self-help outlets for consumers with packaging and in-store displays.

Peddler Sales (a story taking place during the industrial revolution)

The industrial revolution is producing miracles. Water and steam power make it possible to produce goods faster and cheaper. Standardizing products further add to production capacity; still, capital equipment and production processes do not yield their maximum return when only used occasionally. Industrial might must be matched with sales might. Manufacturers begin to take the market to the consumer, either directly or through peddlers. More than ever, sales is about generating demand.

Frank earns his living by filling his wagon with products from the factories along the river and selling them to farmers and rural communities. Most of the people buying Frank's goods have never been to a large city. Much of what he provides, they have never seen before.

Some of the peddlers of Frank's day prefer to keep moving from place to place. They can make more from their persuasive skills on one unsuspecting customer than they can from three who are knowledgeable. On the other hand, these peddlers do not want to meet up with their prey after they feel taken. The objective is to close sales on the day they meet the customer and never see them again.

These peddlers believe ignorance is where the sales are. They use urgency to close deals quickly, insisting they will be the last merchant in the area before the snow comes. They may claim a product is the last of its kind and, of course, another farmer has his eye on it and wants them to come by with it in the morning.

Fear of not purchasing is a common sales objective. Thousands of lightning rods dot the landscape as testaments to the power of the peddler as he spins his web. Ultimately, it becomes apparent that the emperor wears no clothes. Peddlers are viewed by many as wicked swindlers.

Frank prefers to travel through the same towns each year, yet he is concerned about the way he is received. He suspects that earning the confidence and loyalty of his customers is ultimately more profitable than trying to fleece them each time, yet this approach depends on Frank's ability to differentiate his service from that of other peddlers, too many of which are professional con artists.

Today, direct personal selling remains a maligned profession. The distrust remains and there are many alternatives to buying from peddlers. There is little, if anything, one could learn or buy from a peddler that cannot be easily obtained online.

Advertising to Sales (a story taking place in the 1950s)

As technology made it cheaper and cheaper to reach consumers, advertising became a cost-effective way of sending shoppers to the store. The division between advertising and sales was a natural outgrowth of the bureaucratization of developed countries. Advertising was primarily about generating demand. Sales was about closing deals.

Tom makes his living producing ads for the Plymouth brand. Sam sells Plymouths at a local store. In theory, these men are both working to enhance Plymouth sales; however, the two will never meet. In fact, their bosses will never meet, and their bosses' bosses may never meet.

Tom and Sam see the world very differently. Tom sees his role as establishing a brand image for Plymouth, clearly communicating a unique selling proposition for the brand. Sam has only a vague idea what that unique selling proposition is. He doesn't give two hoots about the metrics Tom studies each month, he needs ready-to-buy traffic in the showroom.

In Tom's view, branding delivers more showroom traffic over time. When Tom gets input from those involved with sales, they usually request a push for a sales event. Tom knows 96% of the shoppers watching the TV ads his team puts together are not in market for a vehicle right now, but he also knows he must do what he can to support the sales events.

The two sides learn to live in relative harmony, the advertising driving traffic to the store and the sales teams turning store traffic into sold customers. The sales event occurs entirely face to face with the customer. Sam and other sales professionals listen to the customer, match the customer to the right product, demonstrate the product will meet the customer's needs, and close the sale. Tom and his team share no responsibility in this process.

Today, advertising and sales are viewed as separate functions in most organizations. In some companies, advertising is autonomous and solely focused on branding activities. A common strategy between the two departments may not even exist. In some organizations, advertising serves the sales department, the latter having the upper hand in strategy disagreements.

Sales Integration (a story taking place today)

Most major purchases are researched online before the shopper ever steps foot into a store. Unlike other media, the internet listens, match makes, demonstrates in detail, and sometimes closes the sale.

Mary is a consumer. She spends a portion of her income on commercial-free entertainment, like HBO, Sirius, DVDs, and entertainment downloads from the internet. Mary's mother once wondered how she would know what to buy if it were not for the advertisements on TV, radio, and in the newspaper. Mary wonders how in the world anyone has the patience for all those ads, or why they would need them when all that information is available online.

Mary has a general distrust of salespeople. In her view, they either are not motivated enough to know their product or on commission to lie about their product. Although overly cynical of sales professionals, she is more receptive to what other people say about products online. When shopping online, her product selection is often influenced by reviews from consumers she never met.

When Mary does contact an auto dealership or appliance store, she does so after extensive online research. She knows her alternatives. She knows what she will buy if she does not get satisfaction from the store she contacts. She also knows where she will buy it and what price she will pay. Her transparency into the market makes it very difficult to sell her anything at an above-market price without sound justification and credible documentation.

Mary does not want to be sold anything. She voluntarily enters into sales processes she can control or learn about to avoid feeling fleeced later on. Her sales process generally starts online, yet it will conclude online for some products, at the store for others, and over a chat or phone conversation for others.

What happens between the start and the close is completely unpredictable. Mary may start on a manufacturer's site, then go to a search engine to see where she might want to explore next. She may visit one or more independent sites for information, including which locations offer what she is looking for.

Ultimately, Mary will buy online or transition to a retailer through phone, email, chat, or walking into the store. The choice is hers, and she doesn't do things the same way for all products or even the same way for the same product on another occasion.

Mary controls the sales process. She doesn't give a skinny rat's fanny about advertising or sales. She blocks ads at will and does not hesitate to walk out on salespeople with their competitor's information already in her smartphone. Those companies offering consistent, integrated information across their websites, independent websites, contact centers and stores will be seen as easier to buy from and more apt to earn her trust.

Selling still goes on today, but it generally does not originate with a salesperson. Advertising still plays a role, but obtaining reach and frequency among the most affluent shoppers is more elusive than ever. Organizations operating with autonomous sales and marketing departments can no longer pretend they are consumer centric. Those who look at the market holistically and recognize the infinite number of paths consumers can take toward a sale have the opportunity to integrate their efforts and maximize their sales.

What is Sales Integration?

When shoppers go to websites seeking information about products and services, they deliberately enter a sales process, just as surely as if they were walking into a store. Websites sell. So do catalogs, trade shows, stores, and sales people. Shoppers bounce across all these channels as they buy, so the sales process must work across all channels collectively as well as individually.

Throughout the history of modern marketing, sales and advertising have typically been disjointed. In many organizations, marketing was a separate department from sales. In other words, it was the responsibility of marketing to provide sales opportunities. This method of thinking does not fit in a world of multichannel shopping. The sales process begins online, often on websites with no opportunity to close the sale. Consumers frequently shop across multiple channels before making their purchase. Shoppers decide which channels they want to pull information from, which they want to buy from, and how they want to accept delivery. Businesses must integrate their sales processes to function across all channels in whichever zigzagged approach the shopper takes.

Prior to about 1995, a sales process was generally something that took place at a store. It was often preceded by impressions, influences, and experiences that drove the shopper to the store, but selling itself did not take place until a shopper walked through the doors. Direct marketing existed as a distinct alternative, often in the form of catalogs and direct mail. Any number of frustrations arose for shoppers and merchants alike when store prices and merchandise did not match what was found in the catalogs. Most consumers recognized anything printed was subject to change or discontinuation. Only the stores and call centers could verify an offer and close a sale instantly.

Today, offers are confirmed and sales closed instantly at stores, company websites, shopping websites, auction sites, and via contact centers handling phone, email, and chat communications. Pricing consistency is not sufficient. Product information must be consistent. Shoppers must not only be allowed to change channels, their ability to do so must be facilitated from one to the other, but that's not all. Linked sources of consistent information do not constitute a sales process. Selling must be integrated across the merchant's multichannel marketing network to help the shopper progress to a sale.

Consumers practice multichannel shopping with disregard for the established channels of manufacturers, retailers, and service providers. Distribution channels may be structured, but multichannel shoppers are free to ignore structure and control the sales process, their sales process.

Business can no longer afford to view selling as something one person does to another. Selling is a series of shopping facilitations occurring in an unpredictable sequence toward a transaction that enhances quality of life. Sales efforts are like a series of lily pads. Shoppers hop from pad to pad in their order of choice to go from unmet wants and needs on one side of the pond to satisfaction and delight on the other.

Chapter 2

The Internet Has Ears

Sales starts with a four-step process leading up to the close:

1. LISTEN to the shopper's wants and needs
2. Reach into the firm's portfolio of products, services, and creative solutions to MATCH the shopper with the right bundle of features and benefits
3. DEMONSTRATE, preferably in the shopper's own terms, that the bundle of features and benefits will meet the shoppers needs
4. CLOSE the sale.

Delivery and account management then follow the close.

Discovering the Internet has ears became one of the most eye-opening moments of my career. Through its interactive capability, the internet listens. The ability to listen has two critical impacts on business. 1) It allows the Internet to derive relevance for interruption advertising to a degree that has never been achieved. 2) Listening allows the sales process to begin online.

The Internet listens by essentially saying, "This is all I am going to talk about on this page. I maintain silence until you tell me what you want by typing or clicking on something." The internet listens to absolutes – you click it or you do not. This is first nature for computers, given their binary language. It also listens to text inputs in search tools. This continues to improve, but the internet already surpasses many humans for listening and all humans for information storage.

What a great start toward a successful sale. Sales managers have been saying for decades, "listening is more important than talking, that is why you have two ears and only one mouth." You do not know what the customer's product or information needs are until you listen.

Because the Internet listens, match makes, and demonstrates, the sales process begins online.

The world of marketing is changing fast. The sales process often takes place across a combination of websites and stores. Multiple-channel marketing means selling through a number of channels, like stores and catalogs. This appears easy enough if each individual shopper stays in one channel, though multichannel shopping means the sales process is taking place in several places, and consumers are going wild with multichannel shopping. The adjacent chart shows but one possible stream of shopper activity. We cannot wrestle control away from the shopper, but we can integrate the sales process across these interactive touchpoints.

Multichannel Shopping

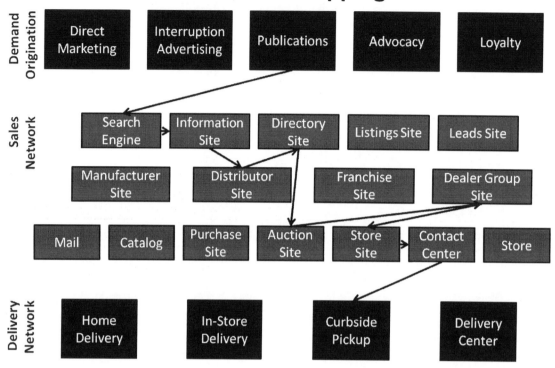

The advent of the internet is not the only thing driving change. An examination of the four P's of marketing – product, price, promotion, and distribution (place) – reveals the following for durable goods purchases:

- A world in which product proliferation is generating more choices than consumers can digest. New feature enhancements emerge between every purchase cycle for virtually every category of durable goods. In fact, many durable goods are discarded prior to becoming physically obsolete simply because they have become functionally obsolete within the ever-demanding, fast-paced environment.
- Prices change rapidly from one sales cycle to another for most durable goods. Many items become cheaper with each purchase cycle due to improved production processes. Improved scale from production, design, and engineering for a global market also push prices down.
- Some promotional resources are being moved from interrupting news, weather, sports, entertainment, or roadside scenery to making product information available when it is requested on websites dedicated to facilitating the shopping process. The relevance of this shift cannot be found in discussions about traditional media vs. new media. What is relevant to the sales process is the distinction between interruption advertising and

permission marketing with ears attached. The former is not part of the sales process, but the latter is.

Across-the-board change is not limited to product sales. Many services are far different than they were a few decades ago. Elder care – like assisted living, hospice, and nursing care – is a different and better product than it once was. It is also shopped for differently, and more changes are on the way. Professional services like legal, medical, and consumer banking now offer tools for self-diagnosing need as well as delivering self-help, yet transitioning to a live professional must always be an option.

Marketers of packaged goods may not feel selling applies to them, but I submit that packaging and in-store promotions constitute selling without the involvement of store personnel. Supermarkets are certainly designed to sell. You want cereal, and sure enough, there is an aisle that says cereal right on it. If you did not know the first thing about cereal, you could categorize them at a glance just by scanning the aisle. The hot cereals are together and segregated from the cold cereals. You want to know which cereals are healthy and which are for kids. That information is made clear by the product names and the artwork on the boxes. You want to know which cereals are most popular, and the amount of shelf space allocated to each product gives you an immediate indication. Which are on sale? Shelf talkers provide the answer.

To some degree, the shopper is having a discussion with the physical store and product packaging.[2] Together, they provide a matching service by answering the shopper's questions regarding where it is, who it is for, how much it is, and which is the best value. Further demonstration of the product is provided on the side of the box. You do not need that information unless the product is in your consideration set. Just like a good salesperson, the box does not try to give you the information until you request the information by lifting it off the shelf and turning the box.

Consumer Packaged Goods (CPG) marketers and the stores retailing their products began replacing sales people decades before the internet came along. The world is a better place for it. Occasionally we need to ask a clerk where to find the Velveeta, but most shoppers are pretty self sufficient all the way to the close. Increasingly, shoppers are taking the close into their own hands as well with self-service checkout.

How did internet shopping catch on so fast? Shoppers already understood how to navigate a sales process sans the salesperson.

---

[2] The communication between the shopper and the store is not truly interactive. Although the shopper reacts to the stores messages, the store does not react to the shopper. This will change over time with monitors on shopping carts connected to a database housing the shopper's information, preferences, shopping list, and previous purchases.

Chapter 3

Multiple-Channel Marketing and Multichannel Shopping

Distribution through multiple channels offers marketers more ways to sell to more people, but it does not necessarily do anything to facilitate multichannel shopping. Walmart is one of those companies operating two nearly distinct distribution channels.

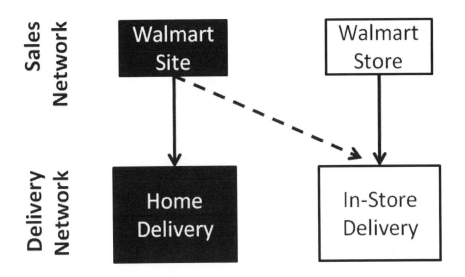

Walmart.com offers many products not available in stores, providing more selection than any single rooftop can, but some of the products available on Walmart.com can be picked up at the store and some cannot. Some of the products on Walmart.com are offered through a Marketplace Retailer and cannot be returned to a Walmart store.

Most impactful of all, the prices on Walmart.com are not necessarily the prices at the store. To its credit, Walmart.com is fairly clear on this point. It is possible for two shoppers to receive delivery of the same product at the same Walmart store at two different prices, the online price and the store price.

When you get right down to it, there is no website supporting Walmart stores. The only thing Walmart.com does for its local stores is provide a locator tool to find them. The stores serve as a delivery point for Walmart.com, but only for select items. In other words, Walmart is a major player in multiple-channel distribution providing almost nothing to facilitate multichannel shopping.

Walmart's key advantage is distribution. It distributes products in the most efficient manner possible, using the savings as a low-cost advantage over competitors. From an internal perspective, Walmart's approach to the internet is consistent with its overall approach to business. However, it is not consistent with the growing expectations of shoppers. Most of Walmart's customers are multichannel shoppers for a wide range of products. They expect the same pricing consistency they receive from other retailers. Indeed, in some states, it is a violation of the law for auto dealers and other merchants to offer one price online and not honor it at the store.

Sears is certainly not the model of sales integration, but they will match prices for all Sears Holdings Company products. There is no need to pay any more from a Kmart or Sears store than through their network of websites.

On BestBuy.com, some of the items include free shipping and some do not. Some are only available in stores. These distinctions are clearly marked when they occur. All items can be returned to the store, whether purchased from the store or online. Any item is available for free in-store pickup. A price match is guaranteed, although there are some limitations. The online product selection can be narrowed to only those items offered through the Best Buy outlet centers. These are the beginning signs of sales integration.

Increasingly, shoppers expect to see some transparency into the store from the website with that store's name in the URL. Sites like BestBuy.com do a much better job of stepping up to the needs of multichannel shoppers than Walmart.com does. Walmart is at a crossroads. It forced thousands of suppliers to comply with its distribution methods, and consumers benefited from the low prices. Will Walmart continue to force its shoppers to accept a store with no online support and a website bearing the store's name with very little linkage to the store itself?

Trusted Advisor Status

Tractor Supply Company offered online tools for shoppers to help determine which product was right for them. The site's Online Welding Guide helped narrow the consideration set of welders. It filtered the various welders by asking the shopper to answer one or more of the following questions:

1. What metals are you welding? (Aluminum, steel, cast iron, etc.)
2. What type of work are you doing? (Maintenance, construction, farm/ranch, etc.)
3. Where will you be working? (Inside, outside, outside in the wind, etc.)
4. How thick is your metal?
5. Are you welding dirty or rusty metal?

The Online Welding Guide listened to the shopper, matched him up with the right welder, and demonstrated the relative pros and cons of each welder remaining in the consideration set. Great retailers have occasionally given this type of advice in stores, but it is simply not possible to do so in store catalogs. Catalogs do not have ears. The sales process started on the retailer's website, and the retailer takes the role of an independent third-party advisor, indifferent to which of the many products carried are purchased.

When retailers carry a wide range of product choices, they can put themselves in the position of trusted advisor to the consumer. This shifts some retailer interests from negotiating bulk deals with a few suppliers based on lowest possible price to carrying a wider range of offerings and maintaining trusted advisor status. Already many retailers carry far more SKUs on their website than are immediately available from any one store. Therefore, the website has a better opportunity to play the trusted advisor role than anyone in the store does.

When asked to rate the importance of custom content and tools on retailer websites, 70% of consumers marked Product Comparison Capabilities either "very important" or "somewhat important."[3] Alternative Product Views received a top-two-box rating from 67% of consumers. Each of these responses came in higher than Peer Ratings and Reviews (60% top-two box). This is not enough evidence to conclude the retail site tools play a more important trusted advisor role to more shoppers than do peer ratings and reviews, nor does the relative importance matter. The results suggest retailers should provide both peer guidance and robust shopping tools in order to obtain trusted advisor status.

Many retailers carrying inventory from a wide range of competing manufacturers find obtaining new site visitors through search turns out to be cost effective. Still, the price of creating shopping

---

[3] *3rd Annual Mindset of the Multi-Channel Shopper Holiday Study*, Lauren Freedman the E-tailing Group, November 2008

tools that enhance the retailer's trusted advisor status may prove to be even more cost effective due to improved conversion rates, greater loyalty, and more advocacy. As site conversion improves, so does the justification for attracting additional site traffic, so one need not come at the expense of the other.

Some stores are stepping up to this challenge by providing kiosks in the store. This brings the entire available inventory into the store, even if many of the products are not physically there. Sales professionals can now become better trusted advisers. Additionally, shoppers can enter into the store for a self-help shopping experience knowing they have not missed anything if they did not consult the chain's website first.

Retailers choosing this strategy will need to find cost-effective ways of increasing the number of SKUs and the number of manufacturer relationships in order to facilitate their trusted advisor status. They will also need to find marketing methods of profiting from their advantage as credible, third-party advisors. So far, the products are being added faster than the shopping tools and value added information is being applied.

Part 2

The Sales Process

Chapter 4

Listening

Advertising shouts at shoppers, but sales is about listening. The internet is the only medium with good listening skills.

Talk about enhanced interactivity for television continues, but little progress has been made. Televisions listen to the remote control, which is still of limited value to marketers. In fact, it usually works against them. The ad starts shouting and the TV channel starts changing. Some viewers even TiVo programs for the purpose of not having to see the ads.

Some radio stations will listen to requests or allow users to call into talk shows yet that does not do much for sponsors trying to sell products. It simply increases engagement with the station or program, the thing the ads are interrupting.

The key to a good radio ad is to make it intrusive – make it stand out from the programming that may have become background noise. When I wrote radio ads, I would brag to clients that I was trying to cause a car wreck. I wanted people to stare at their radio and run into someone. Then I knew I was getting through. In other words, the idea was to draw attention to what I wanted to say about the product. I needed to rise above the status of background noise.

The closest thing my radio ads got to listening was to offer a phone number or some other reference for more information. In other words, the sales process would have to start somewhere else.

Magazine ads do not listen. Neither does direct mail. I read David Ogilvy's book, *Ogilvy on Advertising,* repeatedly with great admiration and put this great man's ideas into action. There is both an art and science to interrupting people's reading. Print ads can do wonderful things to promote products, and they work well when placed in front of the right people, but they cannot listen.

It could be argued that many magazines and mailing lists are finely tuned to a particular lifestyle or demographic, that the advertiser's message is a response to the readers' identifying themselves. Okay, I too sold many direct mail campaigns on that basis. My listening must not have been very good because my response rates were usually only a few percent.

Classified ads provide navigation. "Do you want a car? Now what make are you looking for?" One could argue the newspaper responds with the make section after listening to the fact that you

28

are looking for a car. You might even say that it presents the seller's contact information in response to the shopper having become interested in that particular vehicle. Is it any wonder that newspaper classified ads were once compared to printing money? They were, and to some degree are, the profit engine for newspapers. Advertising in the classified section is not truly interactive, but it is not interruption advertising either. Shoppers go there because they want to buy and products are organized for easy searching.

Of course, this degree of listening pales in comparison to the Internet. Online classified ads are interactive. Shoppers easily scan through millions of vehicles on AutoTrader.com by narrowing their consideration sets with more than a dozen criteria, not just "what make." It is no wonder that the Internet leads more than six times as many late-model used vehicle buyers to the vehicle they buy than do all newspaper and print magazine classified ads combined.[4]

In theory, telemarketing is a great listening medium. In practice, it is often just another form of interruption advertising. It does not listen to find out when it is an appropriate time to have a conversation, and it generally starts out with a long, fast data dump in an effort to spew something out before the listener hangs up. One modern practice is deliberately calling when an answering machine will pick up and transfer the advertiser's recorded message to the prospects answering machine. No listening there.

Interruption advertising plays a critical role in the awareness and interest phases of marketing. This will not and should not stop. In all likelihood, none of these media will be replaced by the Internet or any other form of digital marketing.

What separates the Internet from other media is that the Internet has ears. It listens to shoppers to find out what is important to them. Menu bars dictate as to what the website is willing to listen. A robust site-search tool serves a similar purpose and is preferred by some shoppers. Typically, websites will employ both well-designed menus and site search capability.

Listening has always been the key to sales. Products generally deliver a variety of benefits, and most sellers offer a variety of products. Sellers identify which benefits to present and how best to present them by listening to the shopper. Sales managers have been telling new sales people for many generations that listening is more important than talking.

Those who do not listen well often talk about everything or the wrong things. In some ways, the internet makes personal selling a tougher job than it used to be. Often, shoppers engage a salesperson after previously shopping online. The easy questions have been answered, and standard salesperson chatter about basic features often replicates what the shopper already knows.

---

[4] Source: J.D. Power and Associates' *2008 Used AutoShopper.com Study*, based to buyers of used vehicles with model years 2003-2008.

In a fast-paced world where shoppers have little patience, wasting the shoppers' time on features irrelevant to them and information they already know is not going over well.

Google developed a multi-billion dollar profit-making machine by providing good ears linked to organized information. Google's home page begs the visitor to tell it what they want. Then it gives the shopper additional tools and advice on how to help Google listen better if the results were not as expected.

A few years from now, we will look back on Google's early efforts at listening and wonder how they ever got off the ground, but it was the first huge success in the area of listening. To its credit and everyone's benefit, Google continues to invest in the pursuit, as do competitors. Continued improvement in search is a given, including better ability to search within the website as well as across sites.

In addition to good menus and search, some sites provide links to anticipated tools, answers, or solutions based on where the shopper is on the site and/or what else they have done or asked for on the site. Information about the customer in the company's CRM system may also be used to anticipate information needs.

Offering navigation options based on previous menu selections is similar to asking probing questions. "Since you want one of those, is this category of options of interest to you?" Sales people have been softly probing for information for many years in an effort to help shoppers find the right product for them. This addition to websites will bring about the best online listening ever created.

Chapter 5

Matchmaking

The internet is the greatest matchmaking device ever given to marketers. Amazon is all about matchmaking, as is eBay. Arguably, the most important of all matchmaking is dating services. Many consumers of this service are not choosing an online solution based on cost. The stakes are too high for that. The rapid migration of this industry to the internet is a testament to the quality of its matchmaking ability.

One of the critical skills in matching shoppers with the right product is knowing all the features and benefits of all the products. This is becoming more difficult than ever due to product proliferation. In many product categories, it is not humanly possible to keep up with all the nuances of every offering.

The auto industry offers roughly 300 different models in the United States, and some of those models come in a wide variety of trim packages. Each trim can be further customized with an increasing variety of options. The combinations are mind numbing. There are more different Porsche combinations that can be designed on Porsche's website than Porsche can possibly build in a year.

Automotive websites make it easier for shoppers to design the right vehicle. Some even go so far as to help the shopper find the vehicle of their choice across the inventories of hundreds or thousands of dealers.

Many shoppers are no longer settling for the best vehicle available among a single store's inventory. They want the exact right vehicle. Consumers are frequently upside-down on their vehicle (owe more than it is worth) from the minute they drive it off the lot to more than 3 years later. Since the shopper is going to be saddled with the vehicle for quite some time, the matchmaking portion of the shopping process is critical.

Transparency into market pricing provides a long awaited blessing for the consumer. It has never been easier to get a great deal on a new vehicle, but it has never been harder to find the right vehicle. There are simply too many to choose from without relying on some professional help. Credible, third-party tools can provide help to shoppers and income to those publishers who provide them.

Every year, more consumers turn to independent websites for help in determining which vehicle or vehicle type is right for them. The Consumer Reports model, financial dependence on consumer subscriptions, certainly commands a moral high ground, though publishers have been demonstrating an effective church/state relationship between ad sales and editorial content. There is absolutely no reason why the same cannot be achieved with shopping tools, and in many cases, it is.

From 1995 to about 2005, most automotive shopping tools started by asking shoppers in what make and model they were interested. Research showed many shoppers started their shopping process not knowing which vehicles they should consider.

Today, some sites have car guides helping shoppers identify vehicles particularly relevant for their individual lifestyle. The advertising space adjacent to these tools has derived relevance. The shopper exposed to the ad identifies herself as someone who needs a vehicle like the type the advertiser sells. The website exposes the shopper to the advertiser's vehicle at a time when she is actively looking for vehicle shopping advice. The most valuable advertising opportunities are those with the most relevance. This kind of interruption advertising actually facilitates the matchmaking process.

Shoppers often start their online shopping without knowing what they desire or even what product/service benefits they should be considering. It was Dave Power, founder of J.D. Power and Associates, who taught me if you simply ask shoppers what they want you will find that many truly do not know. This does not mean these shoppers are ignorant or lack the capacity to make decisions. It means they need help.

Initially, most shopping tools were query tools that asked shoppers which option they wanted and/or whether or not they wanted a particular accessory. Product configurators take shoppers down a path that helps them formulate the proper configuration of options and features for that shopper. Modern configurator tools provide links to help.

Matching products to a shopper's lifestyle is but one type of matchmaking tool, yet this can be achieved in a variety of ways. The design of matchmaking tools begins with identification of what information shoppers will be required to input, what will be the basis of the match or mapping, and how the results will be output.

1. Inputs (What shopper information do we need?)
   a. What general type of information will be input or collected from the shopper in order to allow the tool to listen?
   b. In what form will the data be?
   c. How will the data be input?
2. Mapping Source (How will the matching be conducted?)
   a. What will be the criteria for matching?
      i. Expert opinion
      ii. Historical shopping records

         iii.   Historical purchase records

         iv.   Manufacturer intent

   b.   What existing data sources will need to be used to complete the mapping?

         i.   Will the existing data be static (e.g. product specifications, performance or safety rating)? If so, what will be the process for updating it?

         ii.   Will the existing data be dynamic (e.g. interest rates, incentives). If so, how will the tool be linked to the data source?

3.   Outputs (What is the objective of the match?)

   a.   What form of output will most affect the shopper's decision to buy?

   b.   What form of output is best for introducing cross-sell or up-sell opportunities (e.g. new attribute considerations)

   c.   Is it necessary for the output to be transferable or viral? If so, what form is best for that?

   d.   What form of output will shoppers best understand? (e.g. limited results sets, ranking of results sets, a single variable)

   e.   Will there need to be links to additional information?

Inputs

In sales terms, requesting inputs for a shopping tool is like softly probing. Clearly, it does not do much good to probe for information the shopper does not know or you cannot use to help them. Many shoppers are put off by having to answer lots of questions, yet they want some clear direction. Therefore, inputs should be chosen carefully.

Unfortunately, many shoppers begin to select stadium tickets, videos, tools, computers, and the like, only to end the session in frustration. Some sales are going to be lost due to unavailability of the appropriate product or unattractive pricing, nevertheless, sales should not be lost due to difficulty using the shopping tool.

It is amazing to see how many shopping tools related to power equipment (cars, boat, generators, motorcycle, chainsaws) use horsepower as a key input. Yes, some shoppers will have a particular horsepower in mind, but more commonly, shoppers need help understanding how much horsepower they need. The output may be a consideration set of vehicles with sufficient horsepower to get the job done, but the input needs to be the job itself. What job will the machine be required to perform.

If horsepower is used as an input, there must be an immediately available link to information or an additional tool that helps the shopper determine what horsepower is right for them. Often, the best alternative is a two-stage tool that transfers the job requirements into power needs and outputs a minimum power requirement and a consideration set of products meeting those needs. Many shoppers look for this type of shopping assistance. "Based on my needs, what horsepower is best for me, and what consideration set offers that level of power?"

Shoppers often need help determining the right input. Galbraith's law of site design states, "Every decision asked of the shopper requires the immediate availability of information to facilitate that decision." Do not ask what color without showing the colors available. Do not ask how many gigabytes without information on how many gigabytes are recommended for the type of computing the shopper intends to do. Do not ask how many cubic feet of fertilizer without a guide to the recommended amount of fertilizer per acre and a tool for the calculation.

If Galbraith's law of site design is going to be ignored, there needs to be evidence that facilitating information is not required, and that evidence needs to be expressed in dollars, not percentages. It does not matter that 95% of shoppers do not need the additional information or that 99% do not click on the adjacent link to that information. If the gross profit from the 1% of sales that would otherwise be lost is greater than the cost of providing the support by an amount resulting in sufficient ROI, then the support had better be there. Site designers must remember they are working on a sales process facilitating buying decisions. The general manager does not give two flips what percent of shoppers do this that or the other thing. She cares about meeting shopper needs to maximize profitability. It is a business; decisions are made with numbers preceded by a dollar sign.

Once we know what feature or use inputs we are going to ask for, we need to decide how that feature or use will be measured. Some things are measured in absolute terms, either it is there or it is not. "Will the tractor need to power any of these various implements?" "Will the welder be used outdoors?" These inputs can often be collected by asking the shopper to select or unselect a box or radio button.

Other information comes in categories: metal, wood, or glass doors, which type of paint, which type of transmission. These inputs are often collected by displaying a list. It is essential the list of choices be exhaustive. That is to say, no potential answers can be left off the list. Lists are generally most effective in narrowing down the consideration set if only one potential answer is appropriate. Paint and transmissions can only be of one type. If a door of metal and glass is an option, then that combination must be added to the list in order to make it exhaustive.

Many shopping tools involve multiple inputs, requiring multiple decisions of the shopper. The sequencing of these decisions may be important. Price is often a critical variable for decisions regarding individual options and for staying within the limits of overall affordability. It is now common for product configuration tools to display the total price persistently throughout use of the tool, as well as showing the price implications of individual decisions.

Things like power and consumption may need to be collected as a maximum or minimum, at least 100 watts, minimum of 5 horsepower, minimum of 30 miles per gallon. However, power related to most accessories requires precise matching to the attributes of the core product. For example, a 12-volt starter is the only appropriate voltage for a 12-volt system.

When a maximum or minimum is specified, the output will generally result in more than one option. This type of input is most appropriate when the objective of the tool is to narrow the consideration set, rather than generate a single recommendation.

Custom products often require ratio measurement for the input.[5] Window treatments, for example, may require an exact measurement as an input. The shopping tool may use this information to eliminate options not available or appropriate for a particular dimension. If a particular style of shutter is not available for very small windows, then it is appropriate for this input to eliminate this shutter option. The tool could have asked if the window was X inches or smaller; still, we know the exact measurement will be required for ordering custom shutters. Asking for the exact measurement upfront results in one less step and reduced shopper frustration.

Text inputs are common for finding the right website or the right information on a website (search tools), but they are rarely accepted as inputs into a shopping tools. This is unfortunate, but reflects the fact we are still in the early phases of designing online shopping tools.

Mapping Source

Varieties of methods are used to match shoppers with the right products. Some tools match shoppers based on the product features they are looking for as compared to the features available in the product or service. Others try to determine the level of quality, safety, or performances desired from the shopper and match those needs with some professional grading of products across these measures. Some tools try to suggest product consideration sets based on the shopper's lifestyle or personality. Regardless of which activity the shopping tool performs in order to make the match, one of the keys to credibility will be the transparency of that activity.

Some services still prefer a black box approach to how the match is made, "according to our secret formula..." To generate credibility, these shopping tools often rely on testimonials related to results. Providing a list of quotes from previous users in order to build confidence in the black box is an example of using testimonials to mitigate a lack of transparency.

Much has been written about the internet's ability to hold people and organizations accountable for their claims. It appears this is also causing shoppers to demand more complete truthfulness from information sources and more transparency into how conclusions are reached or recommendations based.

---

[5] Ratio measurements have a real zero (e.g. inches, gallons, and speed). Not everything expressed as a number is a ratio measurement (e.g. I.Q. score, temperature, and satisfaction ratings are not ratio measurements)

The value of branding may be diminishing, and there is no doubt about the fragility of that value. A brand name may be trusted by millions of shoppers one day and lose a large segment of those followers the next. A single recall or announcement can have a huge impact. Consider what happened when baby toys were found to contain lead paint, stories about horsemeat in hamburgers, or one day finding out that being Enron's accountant is a stab to the heart. If a brand name is the sole source of your shopping tool's credibility, then the tool will not add to the strength of the brand's credibility, but may take away from it if faulty matches develop into bad publicity.

The internet produces a flood of testimonials and product ratings. Aggregating ratings into "this worked for 73% of people like you" may add credibility to testimonials, or at least make it quick and easy for some shoppers to assimilate the totality of the information.

Which type of shopping tool is best depends on what inputs the shopper is able to provide, what matching methods are attainable, and the credibility of each matching method. There is no one best skill saw, one best computer, or one best motorcycle. The internet allows us to market to the level of one, what is best for the one shopper who is inquiring. The ability to focus in on the needs of a single individual at an interactive touchpoint is what makes this selling rather than advertising.

Economics do matter, as do durability, reliability, size, style, functionality, timeliness, and a host of other possible considerations. Even if a shopping tool listens perfectly – probes for and listens to all the important inputs – it is all for nothing if there is not a good matchmaking system for aligning the shopper's needs with the right bundle of features and benefits.

If we accept the idea that credibility is the most import element of persuasion, then it is important we offer the matching criteria most credible to the individual shopper. The key here is to provide a multitude of credible sources, though some sources may not be valuable to enough shoppers to make each source economically feasible.

The most common shopping tools today are attribute-based. They require the shopper understand the product attributes and know which attributes are right for them. Do you want a sailboat or a powerboat? How long? What size motor or sail?

Automotive Internet started in 1995 by most accounts, and for the first eight years virtually every sight started the shopper off by asking what make and what model they wanted. Many people do not start the automobile shopping process knowing what make and model they want.

Matching shoppers with products or services based on the lifestyle of the shopper and the intended lifestyle of the product can make for a very nice shopping tool.

My wife and I would like to take motorcycle rides into the hills and farm country of Southern Wisconsin. We want the freedom and spontaneity to take dirt roads and even trails to see things off the beaten path. What are all the motorcycles made to be ridden both on and off the road? Which of those are large enough for two riders? Are there any available for under $6,000? Of those, which is the most reliable?

If I walk into the average motorcycle store, what are the chances I will find a salesperson who understands my needs are not the same as either a dirt-bike enthusiast or a street-bike enthusiast? That is the job of selling, online or offline. A good shopping tool that offers comparisons across all relevant brands would help move me from desiring such a bike to owning one. A good tool would listen to my lifestyle, ask the appropriate questions, and line me up with a product that has the right set of attributes, even if I did not start the shopping process knowing what those attributes were.

Outputs

Rarely is the output from a shopping tool sufficient for the shopper's decision making. From a sales perspective, the shopping tool listened to the shopper and offered up one or more solutions to the shopper's needs, but that does not confirm the tool met all the shopper's needs. To get to a close, shopping tools must offer more than query results.

Outputs should be expressed in a way that adds information, allowing for continued exploration into the shopper's needs. In some cases, it should facilitate the opportunity for a close. Every good shopping tool solves a shopping problem, but a great tool points to next possible steps.

What to do with the information may lead to branching: "Your result indicates A may be the best solution; however 20% of shoppers like you also consider B and 10% consider C." Of course, links to information on A, B, and C are essential. Providing a chart or table comparing the three alternatives might show why A is the favored consideration for shoppers like this.

Putting the Matchmaking Tool Together

DiscoverBoating.com provides an interesting tool to help the shopper find the right boat. It begins with a list of ten boating activities. The shopper can select all that apply as their favorites. This query tool narrows the consideration set. The shopper can then select the types of propulsion systems they are willing to consider and/or use scroll bars to select the number of people on board and/or length of the boat. There is also a toggle box to select if the boat must be trailer-able. Each of these query the database of boats to narrow the consideration set.

The shopper can see the consideration set change as she changes her selections, so there is no mystery as to why some boats are recommended and others are not. The tool involves five key variables. After activities, it is difficult to say what order the queries should take place in, so that decision is left to the shopper. It is not necessary to use all of the variables. The shopper can compare up to six boat types.

Unfortunately, the output is little more than a summary of the inputs. This could be modified to present a comparison across the next set of logical variables for consideration. Shoppers can then drill into each category in the consideration set to learn more through text and video. The form for requesting more information generates leads sellable to boat dealers carrying the right product for the right shopper.

The boating industry has so many manufacturers I am not sure it is humanly possible to remember every category served by every manufacturer. Unlike cars, individuals do not ordinarily see hundreds of examples every day. This presents a clear need for such a tool. When a retailer receives a lead from a source like this, the prospect already has an investment in their shopping process and narrowed their consideration set with assistance from a credible source. They are not "just looking."

Other industries, like appliances and elder care are in need of this type of shopping tool and better. What is not needed are more tools asking what brand the shopper is interested in for the purpose of selling the lead to a retailer of the brand. If the shopper already knows that, they can go to that brand's website.

We are moving toward a state of business where shoppers can easily consider a set of competing alternatives without worrying whether they should be considering some they do not know about. This solves a problem that grows each day as product proliferation persists. Great shopping tools will be needed to facilitate this.

Branding is still important. Some shoppers want to buy from Apple so bad they will accept the best set of features from Apple even if another brand would meet more needs or the same needs for less money. Shopping tools within brands are essential.

Even if you know you want an F-150, should you buy the XL, STX, XLT, Lariat, FX4, SVT Raptor, King Ranch, Platinum, or Harley-Davidson model? Ford has a tool that lets the shopper pick up to four of these models. The results are nearly useless. I can tell the SVT Raptor does not come in the SuperCrew cap style and the King Ranch only comes in the SuperCrew. What it does not show is the difference in the interior styling, which is extreme.

Ford does not provide a separate photo gallery for each F-150 model on FordVehicles.com, so making these comparisons takes some tedious hunting. Your loyal shoppers should find it easy to understand as much as possible about your product offerings. Getting them into the right one will help keep them coming back.

Chapter 6

Demonstrating

Some product demonstrations cannot be performed in the store. It is difficult to demonstrate a product of any complexity with a 30-second TV or radio spot. It is virtually impossible on a billboard. On the other hand, the internet gives marketers the opportunity to demonstrate the features and benefits of their products to a degree that has never been known.

Ford produced video for their website showing the frame of an F-150 cut in half, alongside a similar section from Chevrolet, Dodge, and Toyota trucks. The promotion did a fine job of demonstrating the relative toughness of the Ford and reinforced the Ford Tough brand promise. Similar demonstrations were done with the braking system and suspension. These demonstrations were complemented with displays in Ford showrooms.

The internet offers an opportunity to demonstrate product features and benefits in a way that simply was not economically practical in the past. This makes online marketing the right prescription at the right time, because the level of product differentiation in many product categories exceeds anything experienced in the age of mass production.

Several new cell phones are developed every day. Coffee is not a commodity anymore; it is dozens of different bean varieties from around the world. Sodas, soaps, and music players come in a wide range of features, sizes, and even colors. How does a marketer cost-effectively merchandise so many different varieties? The television advertising that made Alka-Seltzer a household word cannot cost-effectively demonstrate the unique benefits of each variety of Alka-Seltzer.

There is certainly a need for an independent, third-party website that gives advice on which pain reliever is right for which symptoms. Imagine if such a site could also locate the product in nearby retailer stocks. It could not only show the sufferer what product to purchase but where to find it. This would be a great place for manufacturers and retailers to advertise the benefits of their products and services.

My view is clear: when shoppers know where to go for shopping advice, the need for branding to the level of becoming a household name is somewhat diminished. However, whether or not a product reaches the brand preference level of a Kleenex, marketers certainly want their product shown in any appropriate consideration set. The fact a shopper seeks advice demonstrates branding alone has not been sufficient for that individual shopper.

When the shopper is looking to find the right product within a brand family, provide tools to help them find the right solution and demonstrate why it is the right solution. All these product differentiations are made for a reason. Matching shoppers to the right product and demonstrating how the product was made just for people like them is selling. The age of "here they are which one do you want?" needs to die quickly. This kind of treatment on a brand site is an invitation to switch to a brand that cares.

The interactive capabilities of the internet can be used to take demonstrations to a new level of confidence building in two ways. First, interactive means shoppers can engage with the product, or a feature of the product, in a virtual way. A virtual test drive may show the movement of the tachometer and then deliver the sound of the engine as the shopper manipulates a virtual accelerator pedal with their mouse or keyboard. Secondly, interactivity means the internet can listen for unmet needs and respond with appropriate product variations, accessories, or alternatives.

An effective salesperson does not go over the top with their demonstration; they continue to listen for shopper preferences not previously uncovered. Shopping sites should be designed the same way. Dynamic personalization provides a means of doing just that. The site can simultaneously demonstrate features known to be relevant to the shopper and probe for additional wants and needs we think the shopper may have.

Probing generally takes the form of additional links on the page. Which links show up is a function of what we know about the shopper. This is based on their activity on the site and with what we know about them in the CRM, combined with mapping founded on logic and/or empirical information from similar shoppers.

The demonstrative capabilities of the internet remain extremely underutilized at this point in time. Marketers have two of the five senses to work with, hearing and seeing. If you do a good enough job with those two, some shoppers may swear they can feel it, taste it, and/or smell it as well. Learning works best when new information ties to long-term memory. Those kinds of associations are much more likely if the marketer employs site, sound, and motion.

Allowing shoppers to explore the product makes perfect sense. Sure, you can have a configuration process that is linear, but it cannot be the only way you allow your shoppers to understand your product.

Sitting through meetings listening to people talk about cutting out shopping content because it is infrequently viewed makes my toenails curl up. Do doctors talk about throwing away the tools they use the least? I hope the surgeon who works on me has the right tool for any eventuality and listens to the signs my body is sending out in order to know what tool needs to be used at what time. Your website needs to be just as surgical and versatile in its selling.

Yes, maintaining site content is a lot of work. So is keeping surgical tools clean and ready. So is selling. Teams designing and managing websites need to step up to the hard work of sales or stay home and play Warcraft, Facebook, or whatever it is that non-business people do with their computers. The office is for business, and business starts with selling.

There will come a day when shoppers can experiment with recipes online. What will the salad look like if mandarin oranges are added? One-quarter cup? Half a cup? How do the black olives on my enchiladas stand out over jack cheese as opposed to cheddar? What will the cookies look like if they are cooked for 9 minutes instead of 10, or cooked at 325° instead of 350°? The internet is capable of providing these demonstrations, yet they are scarcely provided by marketers.

Demonstrating trim differences, options, and accessories is just basic selling. Generally, accessories are poorly demonstrated online. How they will look, how they work, how to install them, and how they make a difference are all important demonstrations. Ford offers a retractable side step for easy access into the pickup bed from the side. Their total online demonstration of this product is a single photo and this text:

> This handy step is positioned under the bed. Available for driver and passenger side. Power coat provides corrosion protection.

That is it. I do not know how high off the ground it will take me, whether it affects ground clearance, or what it looks like when the step is stowed away. I do not have any idea how hard it is to pull it out. The accessory costs $300 and provides a better profit margin (as a percentage) to both the dealer and manufacturer than the truck itself. If I go to the Ford store, the salesperson does not even know the option exists. It seems no one wants to sell it.

I can learn 50 times more about a breakfast cereal by reading the box in the store. I can go to the Cheerios website and find pages of information broken down for new parents, kids, families, or adults. There is no correlation whatsoever between how hard a company works to sell its product and how much it costs.

Marketers must provide better product demonstrations. They also must begin the hard work of benefit demonstrations. I criticize my friends at Ford because they are such a fine company otherwise.[6] It is fantastic that I can spin a CGI image of the Red Candy Metallic Mustang GT Premium Convertible I want with the 402A package. However, shoppers are going to want to see more than the product. They will want to see product benefits. How do I look in the vehicle? How will my things fit in the trunk?

---

[6] Ford now has one of the best Chief Marketing Officers in the auto industry, Jim Farley. Recently, he took over responsibility for parts and sales as well.

On a Japanese website, I saw animated figures on motorcycles varied by gender, height, and weight. That was 2005! CGI technology provides far more opportunities to demonstrate benefits than marketers currently utilize. This in not going to change so long as websites are seen as advertising designed to tease shoppers into visiting the store. Once organizations accept a full recognition that the sales process is starting online, we may start to see more investment in online demonstrations.

Interactivity can be taken a step further by injecting the option of community involvement. Online communities are commonplace with internet games. Players can work together as teams. While these things are cost effective for online entertainment, many marketers and advertising agencies quickly dismiss such advancements as too expensive.

What will the Thanksgiving table look like with Grandma's turkey, stuffing, and gravy; Aunt June's cranberry sauce, and Mom's green bean casserole? When will everything need to be started to make it all come out at the right time? If the whole family is making its plans on the site of a company selling premium turkeys, there is a very good chance Grandma is going to buy that brand.

Today, companies are making a big splash by providing an 800 number for cooking advice on turkeys, but tomorrow's world looks so much better. How high will the spice meter go if I inject an extra tablespoon of Cajun flavoring to my deep-fried turkey? What percent of the adult population finds that level on the spice meter to be intolerable? Do the time and temperature requirements change if I change the basting frequency? What does "done" look like? All this could be seen by all participants in real time.

Shopatron recommends demonstrating the products in use:

> Great brands put product descriptions into a usage scenario. More than simply describing the product, their descriptions detail how an end-user interacts with the product and can provide the appropriate tips necessary for best usage[7]

Hyperlite.com, a Shopatron customer, uses videos to demonstrate their wakeboards in action. The audio portion explains what the board is designed to do and why it is superior in doing it. In some cases, video is also used to demonstrate the production process, providing confidence in durability.

The initial usage challenge for a new user is the boot adjustment, so Hyperlite offers a video on this as well. The shopper knows exactly what she will receive and where she can go for unlimited repeat instruction.

---

[7] *A Branded Manufacturer's Guide to Growing Online Sales*, Shopatron Inc., 2009

Internet games involve countless scenarios with interactivity. They provide stunning and unique results that vary depending on the player's inputs. Probabilities are built into computer football games to simulate the variation in an athlete's performance. Similar techniques can be introduced to account for product variation that includes uncontrollable variables. Miracle Grow cannot simulate the exact growth of your plants. A wart remover cannot demonstrate the exact pace of reduction. Power generation from wind, solar, and other alternative energy sources involves many variables. Nonetheless, it is possible to provide demonstrations of what the results might be as shoppers alter variables. This kind of interactive game can be a confidence-building sales tool.

Greater consumer confidence that the product is right for them is just one positive outcome from a demonstration. Feedback during or after the demonstration can uncover additional wants and needs, or issues that may hinder the sale.

Continuing to listen through the demonstration process is a huge part of selling. Demonstrations on television are infamous for their lack of believability. It is generally assumed a kitchen appliance will not work as well in your kitchen as it appeared to on TV. I think the reason so many advertisers go over the top with their television demonstrations is darkness. They cannot hear or see the shopper and cannot react to their specific wants and needs. This is why TV is no good for sales, although it can work for advertising.

Online, marketers can build sites that listen to shoppers, and then listen to the click-stream to help determine where the listening is not working optimally.

Any car salesperson will tell you some shoppers come into the store intending to buy one thing and drive home in another. Generally, someone listened to the shopper and realized, often during the demonstration process, the matchmaking was not right.

Many shopping tools use a funnel approach, continually narrowing down the consideration set with no possibility to reverse direction other than starting over. Not only do the tools not listen, they work to keep the shopper from doing what they so naturally do, discover. Watch people shop in stores. They often bounce from one product to another and back again. They might discover a new feature and wonder if that other one had it and they just did not notice. They think of new uses and wonder if the other one would be good for that as well. They see shortcomings and check that concern against other alternatives.

Discovery is the most natural way of learning. Put any two year old in an environment they have never been in before. They do not sit and evaluate what to play with; they go right at something. Then they notice something else. Then they are back to the first thing. They act like little pinballs, and so do many shoppers.

Advertising is nearly always linear. Radio and TV spots go from start to finish. Jingles go from start to finish. Text goes from start to finish. Shoppers do not interact with ads; they are taken through them in a linear fashion. The communication is one way. Sales processes, on the other hand, are not linear. There may be guidelines, steps, and even scripts, but constant listening and the ability to react are what distinguish selling from advertising.

Great sales people facilitate the discover process. Great sales people rejoice when they discover a mismatch in the discovery stage. Now they have a chance to provide an alternative match and start over on the demonstration to get to a close. The old path was not going to work, so the salesperson backs up to find a new path that will work.

Advertising is a numbers game. No linear path works for everyone in the target market, so you do the best you can to move the maximum number possible to the next step. In sales, the number is one. Sales people with a set procedure to jam the shopper through often burn through store traffic one after another. Listening, flexibility, and facilitation of discovery are essential to great selling. The same is true with the online sales process. Listening online is possible during and after the demonstration. Doing so provides a much better opportunity for a close.

Integrating the sales process often means listening for when the shopper needs to transition from the online shopping process to the offline process. I recall working with a number of auto manufacturers on their product configurators. Problems often arose when shoppers picked two or more options that did not go together. Essentially, the problem was finding the best way to jam the shopper through the configuration process when they want a bundle not offered, but the objective of manufacturer websites is to make contact between the shopper and a store.

As I look at the problem today, through the lens of sales integration, the problem is an opportunity. What a great time to give shoppers an opportunity to call or chat with an expert who can better listen to why the shopper is considering items that don't go together and offer a creative solution to the root cause. Sometimes, a website needs to listen for when its own listening skills may not be sufficient.

Chapter 7

Transitioning from Online to Offline

Salespeople must adapt just as surely as websites do. There was a time when salespeople could frequently get away with treating consumers as though they did not know how to buy, but that time passed. I knew people in the automobile and mobile home industries who greatly preferred uninformed shoppers. The logic was simple; if you can get twice the gross profit from a sale to a uniformed shopper, why bother with the hard cases.

There is no shortage of fools in the world. This is something I think we can put in the file labeled, "things that will never change." Unfortunately, pulling the wool over shopper's eyes will never die out as a way of making money. Nevertheless, most of the wealth is in the hands of people who know how to obtain the information they need before making purchases. However one defines and measures the pool of informed shoppers, it continues to grow in size and capability.

There should be no doubt this will continue. Google's mission is "to organize the world's information and make it universally accessible and useful." What a brilliant business model for relevant advertising. Some of that information relates to products, including price. This force is narrowing the range of negotiated prices. Price discrimination simply does not deliver the same returns it used to before information became so readily available.

This is not one of those pendulum shifts that will come back at some point in time. Negotiation today is more about working together toward an agreement that maximizes quality of life for both participants. The win-lose approach to negotiation depends upon one party possessing significantly more information, power, or time than the other. The internet provides more information about the other party, and more information about alternatives. It is hard to exercise power over a customer or supplier if they have transparency into the market revealing better alternatives to your offer.

In 1986 I found myself shopping in a Chrysler/Plymouth store because the manufacturer advertised a very low finance rate for 24-month loans. I knew this rate was a tease, aimed at people who probably would baulk at the payments on a short-term loan and opt for something longer, but this was exactly the kind of loan I wanted. In other words, I was sold on the loan and looking to see if Plymouth had a vehicle that met my very utilitarian demands. As luck would have it, a match was found. I had only a vague idea about how much below the MSRP I should be paying and the negotiating process was the only method I had for finding out. The sales manager became frustrated with my negotiating tactics and revealed his displeasure the public school system did not teach young people how to buy a car. As someone who had not only bought vehicles before but had sold them for a living, I was more than a little insulted. Nonetheless, it was easier to get over the insult from this sales manager than to start the nasty process with someone else at another store with the high likelihood of similar result.

Today, most consumers start their engagement with the salesperson after going deep into the shopping process online. They often know the MSRP, the invoice price, and the target price provided by independent sites like Cars.com and Edmunds.com. They have the price of nearly every competing vehicle on the smart phone in their purse. They not only know how to shop for a vehicle, they have been doing it online for weeks or even months. The person most in the dark is the salesperson. The consumer invested countless hours in the sales process, and the salesperson just now got invited to the party.

That sales manager from 1986 has either transformed his ways, retired, or is about to get retired by an army of consumers now in control of their individual shopping processes. Competing vehicles are 1/4th of an inch away on the consumer's hand-held device. Many automotive sites list over 3,000,000 vehicles, easily sorted and available on the screen.

People are the most adaptable machines in business. They are capable of adjusting to the new environment of sales integration where the sales process starts online but finishes with them. However, many sales processes are already being carried out completely online, and self-help shopping tools for consumers will continue to improve dramatically. If salespeople cannot adapt to sales integration they will ultimately be displaced by online systems and automated delivery processes.

When shoppers come to the store for durable goods, high fashion, professional services, or other expensive items, it is important sales personnel recognize them for the well-informed online shopper they probably are. Listening involves asking some softly probing questions to uncover more wants and needs of the shopper. One of the early probes must involve asking the shopper what they have seen online and what they liked.

For expensive, complex products and professional services, initial offline contact between the shopper and the store often takes place via phone, email, or chat. In many cases, it is just not possible to produce a website that answers all the shopper's questions, yet many shoppers want answers before they are willing to meet face to face.

In most cases, the person answering the phone or chat knows darn well the shopper has been on line, or is online during the conversation. Most experts agree it is vital those answering the shoppers' calls have the store's website and/or company website up on their monitor before the call. If information about your store, service, or inventory is available on other websites, they need to be open as well. This is as basic as it comes. Looking at the same thing the shopper does leads to a much richer conversation.

For most of us, talking on the phone is a much better form of communication than talking in text. The shopper's tone of voice carries a great deal of information that is hard to get with text. Once again, the shopper is in control of how the communication will take place, and visual-only communication is here to stay. According to Contact At Once, the leading chat provider in the auto industry, the peak time for auto shoppers to chat with dealerships is afternoons during the week. Often, it is not possible or appropriate to shop on the phone at work, but millions of Americans shop online during work hours. Those dealers still not using chat are losing business to those who do use it.

Some shoppers still prefer to email their questions. Email is particularly beneficial when the shopper knows it will take considerable time to formulate an answer to their question. It is best to answer the shopper right away with a personalized (not auto response) confirmation that their question is understood and an answer is being developed.

Providing maps and directions boosts walk-in traffic. Making it easy to print or download merchandise details and store details also helps. These same printouts and downloads may be shared with decision makers and influencers, so they should be designed with all of the care and thinking one would put into any other piece of sales material.

Chapter 8

Close

When I began writing this book, my thought was the majority of durable goods sales would close at the store, even though most of them begin online. My research does not support my original hypothesis. Sites like CompactAppliance.com already sell directly to the public with sales people as chat and phone support only.

Amazon sells professional video cameras for over $5,000. Between the product information on the site and the customer reviews, many of us do not feel the need to sit down with a commissioned salesperson to make the decision. In some cases, the shopper can even download a PDF version of the product manual before making the decision. The relevant accessories are all right there, along with helpful comments from people using the product. Many of us will never talk to another electronics salesperson for the rest of our lives. Too many of them were simply clerks to begin with.

Cutting out the salesperson is far more likely to be the case with white goods and electronics than for houses and cars. The amount of money being spent makes a huge difference. Many shoppers need a sensory experience – touching, smelling, and feeling – before making a large purchase. Additionally, manufacturer and retailer websites are a long way from being able to meet the information needs of most shoppers. Still, sites will improve and sales people must as well. Most of all, sites and salespeople must be made to work together.

There is some likelihood professional selling for cars and homes will split into two service levels:

1. Value-adding salespeople
2. Low-skilled clerks who simply facilitate the sensory experience, test-drives and walk-throughs, and leave the bulk of the sales experience to interactive media, online and inside the store.

There are over 1,000,000 Realtors in the United States. Many of them are genuine experts. Some of them are about as sharp as a potato. The best thing they can do is be on time with a key. The fact these two groups share the same title is a shame.

The same is true of automobile sales people. Many of them leave their customers extremely satisfied. They know their product and know how to uncover the customer's needs. Like real estate, just about anyone can get into the business of selling cars. Each year, thousands of duds come in and out of the business, further polluting its reputation. Some of the worst offenders are the five-car Fred types[8] who barely sell enough vehicles to stay in the business, pay the space rent on their trailer, and keep themselves in cigarettes.

In the case of white goods, it is hard to find true sales professionals. Does anyone really think the Sears salesperson has any idea which machine will last longer or get clothes cleaner? Interactive tools, both inside the store and outside, are undoubtedly better equipped to help consumers make cost/benefit tradeoff decisions and are one heck of a lot cheaper.

I include myself in this criticism. At the age of 18, I was a terrible car salesman, and did my share of polluting the industry with my approach. I often threw customers what I thought was such a good line before understanding their needs. The fact is, anyone can say, "If I could make you one heck of a deal, would you buy the car today?" Not everyone can get the shopper into the right vehicle and help them understand how it will meet their needs.

Within some department stores, scanners allow shoppers to check prices themselves and even checkout on their own. Some stores are using in-store kiosks as a way to facilitate more SKUs than can be carried in the store. Many are finding a split between shoppers using the kiosk to buy and those putting items in a shopping cart and purchasing online at a later date. The success of the kiosk should not be measured by sales through either the internet or the store. Rather, it should be measured by its contribution to the integrated sales effort.

The link to professional sales help for in-store shoppers may come from shoppers using their internet-enabled devices within the store to link with the store's website. If this transition takes place, companies like Walmart must move toward greater integration between the site and the store. In the June, 2010 edition of *Internet Retailer*, Senior Editor Thad Rueter reported that Walmart intends to make multichannel integration a strategic priority over the next five years.

For some industries, it is impossible to tell which will become dominant, kiosks or smartphones. In others, there is no question about it. Some automobile dealerships provide in-store kiosks and some provide desktop computers for consumer use, but every store now experiences shoppers walking through the store comparing vehicles on the lot to those they find on their smartphone.

The point of greatest advantage for auto dealers is the Finance and Insurance (F&I) desk. Margins on warranties, security systems, gap insurance, and the like are high. The smartphone is making its way into this stage of the sales process as well.

---

[8] Five-car Fred is an industry expression for a salesperson barely selling enough vehicles to get by. The sales commission from five car sales per month varies but generally does not provide a high standard of living.

In other retail settings, shoppers may feel more trusting of the store and prefer the advantages of a larger screen. There may even be an upsell effect as other shoppers look over the kiosk user's shoulder with envy.

Too often, half-hearted interactive efforts substitute live people in the name of cost savings. This most often occurs in non-sales situations, like museums, where an administrator attempts to check a box in the cheapest way possible. The consequence of these systems may be a poor impression on interactive systems, leading to a greater reluctance to implement them in sales environments within the store. Savvy marketers will need to look past the empirical evidence provided by poor execution and envision what is possible.

The ability to close remains as important as ever. Improvement continues to be made in shopping carts. In general, they are not where they need to be, but the problems are attracting resources. Improvement also must continue among sales professionals. Overcoming objections, recognizing when to stop with the upsells, and knowing when to switch products for a better fit are all skills people should be able to do better than software for years to come. However, each generation of software builds on what was learned from the previous generation. That is not happening as well as it should with people. There will be fewer sales people in the future. Those who remain must be better invested in than ever with outstanding training and continual updates to training.

Chapter 9

Delivery

Any good salesperson knows selling does not stop with the close. There are five profit-generating objectives that come with the delivery of a product or service: payment, loyalty, advocacy, cross-sell, and upsell.

Being paid is something that cannot be taken for granted once the deal closes. Sales can unwind in a variety of ways, from payment failure to legal action. Some industries are bound by law to allow deals to unwind after delivery. In today's world of online ratings, many businesses find it more profitable to let a deal unwind than to have thousands of other shoppers read about it online for the rest of eternity.

Great delivery can make all the difference in whether or not a deal unwinds. Assuring products arrive on time and intact does not cover the ante. Delivery does not mean putting the product in the shopper's hands. Businesses must make sure the shopper can begin taking delivery of the product benefits as soon as possible.

Fantastic delivery either provides a positive or eliminates a negative. Product managers must think about what additional benefits can be generated at the delivery stage and how the cost of providing each one stacks up with the financial benefits from one or more of the five profit generating objectives.

For premium products, great delivery can generate additional profits in many of these five ways by reinforcing the brand promise. Consider a line of premium dairy products. Imagine if when the customer's Peapod delivery arrived a refrigerator thermometer strip was included – with the dairy company's logo of course – along with a note complementing the shopper on their selection of the finest dairy products. The note would work to inform the shopper of both the added taste and health benefits associated with keeping premium dairy products at the proper temperature, and demonstrate increased shelf life. This customer is more likely to buy the brand again, more likely to recommend the brand, more likely to begin purchasing all their dairy products from the brand, and more likely to move up to a super-premium product from the brand if it is available or becomes available.

Eliminating worry is a negative eliminator. Goods that require assembly come with a built-in anxiety factor that often lingers until the product is assembled, in place, in use, and sufficient use has been experienced to generate confidence that the product will continue to deliver the expected benefits for the expected period.

Payment

In high school, I put all of my bets on making it into the United States Air Force Academy. I qualified and even received the required congressional nomination, but I was not admitted. For a variety of reasons, I eventually chose to be self-supporting and put myself through college at the same time. I sold door-to-door and even sold cars at the age of 18. I sold men's clothing for Montgomery Ward and washed dishes in their cafeteria for extra hours.

My big break came when I landed a job as a field collector for Sears Roebuck. At the time, Sears was the nation's leading retailer and its credit card was number one, as well. If customers did not make their payments, someone called them on the phone. If that did not work, a field collector came knocking on their door.

The collector has no power to make anyone pay. Getting the collector off the customer's porch needs to be seen as a substantial benefit. Doing this in South Central and Southwest Los Angeles was risky business, but the job paid considerably more than I had been earning, and I was determined to do it.

Later, I collected for Southern California Gas Company. There I had power. If you do not pay after one warning, someone like me shuts off the gas to your home. You get to think it over in a cold shower. If your business is a restaurant or dry cleaner, you are out of business the moment your gas is shut off.

The lessons I learned as a bill collector continue to serve me well today. Consumers are broke when they are out of cash, not when they are out of income. The same is true of businesses; cash is king. You absolutely need to get paid and keep the deal from unwinding.

Delivering a quality product helps to assure payment, but the definition of product quality has changed. While I was at J.D. Power and Associates, we learned that high quality was not just the fewest possible malfunctions per 100 vehicles. Quality also meant shoppers knew how to extract the benefits they desired from vehicles that were becoming increasingly complex. Too many automobile sales people stop at the close and send buyers driving off in vehicles they do not know how to operate.

In the early years of the iDrive[9], more than one BMW sale unwound because consumers came back to the store in complete frustration over the system. The ease of using the system has been improved, but the importance of teaching the customer how to use the system during the delivery has not diminished.

Leasing companies would be wise to adjust their terms based on the delivery process and ease of using the product. Nearly all consumers have the money to pay someone. Generally, the last companies on the list are the ones with the poorest delivery. Consumers do not walk away from the lease on a product they know how to extract full value from. The first thing they abandon is the product they do not know how to use sufficiently.

Services with monthly fees or automatic renewals must be sure their customers receive full value. The security company installing a system the customer still cannot operate properly is going to suffer from more customers stopping payment prior to contract fulfillment than a company providing great delivery to prevent this.

Loyalty

In many sales, delivery is the last touchpoint before the next shopping cycle. This touchpoint can determine how the consumer recalls the tone and culture of your company. It can also determine how quickly the consumer begins to experience the full benefits of your product.

It is becoming commonplace for major department stores to offer in-store pickup of orders purchased online. Sending shoppers to the back of the store to pickup items at a counter where no one is working does not enhance loyalty. Shoppers who already made their purchase and have not yet had an opportunity to see or touch it should be treated at least as well as those who are thinking about it and looking at it. Of course, that would not be the thinking of a slick store manager focused only on today's sales, but it must be the attitude of any store looking to earn repeat business.

Sears Holdings Corporation is experimenting with MyGofer. At their store in Joliet, IL, shoppers do not even need to get out of their vehicle. They can drive through, and store personnel will load the products they ordered on MyGofer.com into the vehicle. There are varieties of reasons why people do not want to get out of their vehicle and go into the store. Weather can be particularly difficult on people who are moving slow or are awkward in their walking, due to age, handicap, or a recent injury. Getting three small children in and out of car seats, in and out of a cart, and safely back and forth across a parking lot is a major shopping deterrence. The challenges of

---

[9] iDrive is the dashboard unit integrating a number of systems, including navigation, communications, and entertainment.

managing in-store behavior when small children outnumber you can lead to feelings you never knew you had and never want to have again. Some people do not want to come into the store because of their appearance at the time. Automobiles are like safety zones. It does not matter how you smell or if you spilled sauce on your shirt, you are comfortable in your vehicle in a state that would not be comfortable in the store. Sears Holdings Corporation offers MyGofer counters within traditional retail facilities. These counters now exist in over 150 Kmart stores, and some even provide curbside pickup.

When products are shipped to the customer, it does not matter whether you contract out the shipping of your product or do it yourself. How it is delivered will impact the image of your company. You can have the best packaging in the world, but if it is smashed up by the time it gets there, you are going to have trouble getting the next purchase. Customers do not want broken parts replaced; they want everything right the first time.

For products requiring assembly, product quality is only as good as the instruction manuals and the skills of your do-it-yourself customers. You only get to control one part of this vital combination, so you had better put your best foot forward. Is the tone of your instruction manual that of an engineer checking the box to say "I told them how," or does it sound like someone who wants the shopper to enjoy the product they are so proud of and come back for more?

If you want to take your delivery to the next level, ask a few sales people or marketing experts to put your product together using your existing instructions, then ask them to tell you what changes you need to make in order to start earning repeat business. Most instructions appear to be written by people who are bothered by the fact they need customers.

At RevenueGuru.com, we are experimenting with interactive instructions. These online programs will be available for viewing at any time, including prior to purchase. These flash programs can branch off into different languages and different experience levels. Photos and videos can be used for critical parts of identification and complex assembly steps.

Advocacy

When I talk about extraordinary delivery, I am referring to a level of delivery service that modifies the brand image in a very positive way. Many companies use the term extraordinary delivery as a warning that some delivery circumstances, the extraordinary ones, will result in increased costs. Being compensated extra for an extra level of service is fair, but it does not lead to advocacy from your customer to the hundreds of friends who just read your customer's post on Facebook. If the arrival of a product significantly enhances quality of life, then it just might be worthy of a post. If the delivery of the product brings about more positive excitement regarding the product than anticipated, that may also be worth posting. If the delivery of a product generates deep gratitude toward the retailer or manufacturer, it may be a story worth telling for the rest of their lives.

Companies spend millions of dollars advertising to the friends and neighbors of their customers. Yet, when they have a chance to thrill their customers to such a high degree that the customer will become an advocate for the brand, the focus is on cutting costs and extracting additional revenue.

This is not how Carl Sewell's organization delivers cars and trucks. Mr. Sewell literally wrote the book on customer service for auto dealers. His stores sell the same vehicles his competitors sell, yet his customers are happy to pay a premium for his products and recommend their friends and families do the same. Premium delivery is standard for the Sewell organization.

Some products are a one-time purchase for most of the shoppers buying them, which is even more reason to deliver the product in a way that will stimulate advocacy. This is particularly true for premium products or specialty goods that beg the question, "Where did you get that?" You want the answer to that question to include lots of flowery adjectives and adverbs regarding your product, people, website, and delivery.

Your delivery can say, "you bought it here it is," or "you bought us here we are." The former does not want further communication, usually thinking that communication adds cost and allows deals to unwind. The latter encourages communication to the company and about the company.

Many of those jumping on the social media craze amaze me. Social media is a great thing. However, if one side of your business is attempting to get as many Facebook fans and Twitter followers as possible, while the delivery of your product comes across cold as ice, your sales process is not integrated. Businesses need to get right on the fundamentals of doing business before they allow themselves to become worked up about the latest bright, shiny object. Few things could be more fundamental than delivering your product in a way that encourages your customer to become your advocate.

If the delivery is going to have complications, it is best to let the shopper know what to expect. Little Cottage Co. sells premium playhouses for children. Their website, CottageKits.com explains what the delivery options are and what will be required of the shopper at the time of delivery. Photos are used to show what it will look like when the truck pulls up with a pre-built unit. There is also a section, complete with pictures, on site preparation.

The buyer is not always the user. For example, many products purchased online are gifts. Premium delivery should be sold as a benefit to the buyer and as an enhancement to user satisfaction. Wouldn't it be great if grandma did not have to lug that birdbath you sent her from the driveway to the backyard? That gives the buyer a better feeling about the gift they sent. The user instantly develops more appreciation of the product, resulting in more advocacy.

Sam's Club offers several levels of delivery, from dropping it at the curb to placing the item in the customer's room of choice. Their website does a decent job of defining each level of service, but does nothing to sell them. There are no pictures of what delivery will look like or smiles on the faces of those watching Sam's Club's white glove level of service take place on their behalf.

Contracting the shipping does not let a business off the hook for delivery of the promised benefits. Companies taking in millions or billions of dollars for products delivered to the shopper's home need to do some research on how well the delivery is meeting customer needs. I am not talking about research like Amazon's, "Was the box size and packaging appropriate for the items? Too Small, About Right, Too Big, Way Too Big." This is not research; this is a thinly veiled attempt to limit Amazon's accountability for delivery.

Everyone involved in the delivery of your product or service should be required to read *The Oz Principle* and begin taking accountability for exceptional delivery that is in harmony with the rest of sales process. Web intelligence from companies like J.D. Power and Associates and Nielsen make it easier than ever to measure the buzz taking place online about your products and your company. Are any of these metrics part of the Key Performance Indicators (KPIs) for those who are involved in your product delivery? They should be.

Cross-Selling

The term cross-sell has many meanings. Throughout this book, I limit the term to the practice of obtaining additional business from the same customer for non-complementary goods. When Amazon.com points out that people who bought the book you are buying also bought this other book, it is cross-selling. Reading one book will not help you read the other, but people with similar habits as you sometimes buy both.

Customers who buy nutritional supplements are far more likely to buy books about them than those who do not. Of course, the reverse is true as well. The delivery of one should include an offer of the other.

If a customer buys a particular kind of hot sauce, then other spicy sauces should be introduced upon delivery. The second hot sauce does not complement the first. They do not go together. However, the first sale tells us something about the shopper's taste. Offering variety around that taste is welcome marketing.

Upselling

An example of upselling is when you select a $399.99 computer on Amazon.com and it says for $526.89 you can get the computer with a LCD monitor and a super high-resolution cable. Upselling gives the shopper an opportunity to move up to a better product or bundle.

Some products, like automobiles, motorcycles, boats, and ATVs can be upgraded after the purchase. Most automobile accessories are not purchased with the vehicle. The lion's share is purchased later and often not from the same dealership that sold the car. Part of the delivery process should be to help the customer identify the telltale signs that an additional accessory would enhance their quality of life. That might sound like, "If you do decide to start taking your bicycles out to the beach area, we can get you the exact bike rack that was made for this vehicle within 48 hours."

Another form of upselling is providing service along with the product. Delivery of virtually every do-it-yourself package should include a professional way out. Some of your do-it-yourselfers are bound to be biting off more than they can chew. Providing a professional service option can enhance customer satisfaction as well as provide additional revenue. More on this subject is provided in the chapter on Horizontal Sales Integration.

If your business cannot profit from the sale of complementary services, sell leads or ads to those who can. If you cannot sell leads or ads for complementary services, then provide the service free. The service providers you refer your customers to will speak highly of your product or risk being cut off. There is always something to be gained by providing easy access to a more holistic solution.

Sites like WhiteHouseBlackMarket.com suggest the appropriate earrings, shoes, and undergarments to go with the dress the shopper is considering. Knowing how the entire ensemble is going to come together can increase close rates for the core product and sell accessories.

Chapter 10

Account Management

"Why do I only hear from you when you want to sell me something?"

Online account management dramatically changed the insurance and financial services industries. If your product is intangible, chances are you are never going to see some of your customers again. I have been inside a bank four times in the past five years. Three of those times I needed something notarized. I have a six-figure saving account with people I have never met, and a mortgage from a company located somewhere I have never been. I may be a bit unusual in this regard, but the scenario becomes increasingly common with each passing day.

In many respects, companies with no tangible products have it easy. Either they get good at managing and growing relationships online, or they die. The bigger challenge is for companies who do see their customers. Many of these companies remain asleep at the wheel.

If you see me in business attire, I am wearing clothes from a Brooks Brothers outlet store. Other than sending me a card or email to notify me about a sale, I have no relationship with Brooks Brothers outside of their outlet stores. If there is a new shirt pattern or a new set of ties available, I do not know about it. Frankly, my career would probably benefit from me spending more money at Brooks Brothers than I do, but we do not have a relationship outside of the store, and I hate shopping. This retailer could increase their sales by providing better account management.

This is far from an isolated situation and needs to be addressed by more organizations. Some companies offer Personalized URLs (PURLs) to their shoppers. Another method is to provide shoppers with a personal account on a destination site.

ChannelNet develops PURLs and a secure site for every customer with a lease from BMW, which is provided 180 days before termination of the lease. At any time, the customer can view their account, schedule a lease-end inspection, see special offers on a new BMW, and check the terms and remaining length of their lease. The benefits to BMW are numerous: more service business, higher resale values if products are maintained properly, and a closer relationship with the shopper leading to higher loyalty and advocacy.

Sears enjoys the patronage of thousands of loyal Craftsman shoppers. Prior to the internet, it had no way of knowing who needed to know when they launched a new line of cordless tools or a new table saw. ManageMyLife.com is an initial effort at engaging customers with what is available from Sears and how to get the most from their products. Consumers can download product manuals, ask questions, view project plans, and organize their list of Sears products. It is certainly a step in the right direction.

If social media is primarily about building loyalty and advocacy, then a store locator on a company's Facebook page, or a link to one, makes a great deal of sense. Social media can be helpful for facilitating advocacy to friends in far-off markets. Giving your customers an opportunity to help their friends into the sales process is an important part of integration.

Part 3

Vertical and Horizontal Sales Integration

Chapter 11

Introduction to Vertical and Horizontal Sales Integration

The chart below shows how many different types of touchpoints may exist for a single product. Adding further complication, solutions are often not derived from a single product. Integrating the sales process across all of these touchpoints for just the core product may not be enough. In some cases, the sale of financing, warranties, service and complementary products may also need to be integrated across these touchpoints.

Sales Integration

Products	Services	Warranties	Financing

Demand Origination

Direct Marketing	Interruption Advertising	Publications	Advocacy	Loyalty

Sales Network

Search Engine	Information Site	Directory Site	Listings Site	Leads Site

Manufacturer Site	Distributor Site	Franchise Site	Dealer Group Site

Mail	Catalog	Purchase Site	Auction Site	Store Site	Contact Center	Store

Delivery Network

Home Delivery	In-Store Delivery	Curbside Pickup	Delivery Center

Account Management

PURLs	Online Accounts	Contact Center	Store

Like pin-balls, shoppers bounce up and down, and side to side through the touchpoints in various stages of the sales process in any number of combinations. The objective of sales integration is not to identify the most common paths for each industry, but to develop a network of touchpoints that contribute to the sales process for each shopper's needs.

For simplification, the discussion is split into two sections:

1. Vertical Integration, the points of demand origination and the variety of touchpoints through the sales process.
2. Horizontal Integration, the variety of products and services that may be needed to deliver a comprehensive solution.

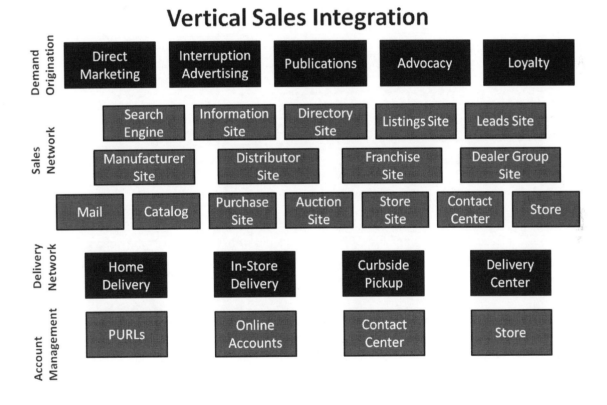

Horizontal Sales Integration

	Products	Services	Warranties	Financing
Demand Origination				
Sales Network				
Delivery Network				
Account Management				

The list of interactive touchpoints is not meant to be exclusive. Nor is it the mission of this book to provide ridged definitions and distinctions. Individual websites are constantly changing and new business models are constantly being developed. The objective here is to provide a framework for thinking about the growing number of touchpoints involving sales activity.

The following chapters go through the various points of demand origination and the touchpoints contributing to the sales process. This discussion is followed by a look at how to integrate the sales process across these points. Next, we will take each element involved in horizontal integration, followed by a look at how these can be addressed comprehensively.

Chapter 12

Demand Origination

Demand is driven in a variety of ways. While demand origination is often non-interactive, it is important to understand what causes demand in order to understand the interactive touchpoints that follow.

Loyalty and Advocacy

The best demand generator is often the product itself. Experiences with the product can come through ownership, renting, borrowing, or simply observation. In the case of services, the experience may be direct or observing the benefits derived by the service.

Increasingly, social media is enhancing opportunities for both loyalty and advocacy. Some customers identify themselves with their products through social media. Their pictures may include them with their motorcycle or in a shirt with their favorite recording artist on the front. They may post about their product use. This type of identification with the product can strengthen loyalty. It can also generate advocacy.

Brand or store participation in social media can facilitate the spread of loyalty and advocacy. If a loyal customer knows your brand has a good Facebook page, this might make him more apt to send a friend or family member to that page. There can be a big difference between. "Thanks, I like it too." and "Thanks, I like it too. Here is a link to that company's Facebook page." The latter is true advocacy, suggesting a purchase be considered.

A brand or store's social media effort can involve directly contacting customers to strengthen their loyalty and stimulate advocacy. It can be news or information relevant to the product, brand, product category, or lifestyle. This is a more subtle approach to building loyalty and the propensity to refer. Social media can also passively serve as a readily available source of information when the time is right.

There is no one best approach to the use of social media. The right course depends on the brand or store's relationship with its customers, its culture, and the frequency of product use. However, no debate exists regarding the newfound opportunity to enhance advocacy and loyalty through social media.

Publications

News still drives demand. Earned media in both online and offline publications can be a big boost for new products or existing products with exciting new features.

Consumers don't just view, listen to, and read news for information about the things impacting their lives. They want to know what they can do to enhance their quality of life. Often, that includes new product offerings. Many consumer products are obsolete before they wear out. Consumers often learn through news sources important product information sending them back to market, rather than just waiting until their current product is inoperable.

News about the product or store can also link back to your store's website. If the home page is the landing page for those links, make sure it has the information people from that news article will be looking for. For example, if your new product launch is news worthy, make sure a clear link to information about that product is available on the home page. Later, the product link may be found under a product category menu. For now, it should be more exposed if possible. New site visitors often bounce if they don't immediately see what they are looking for.

The same is true in the physical store. If positive news has been generated about the store, make it clear to arriving customers this is in fact the store they read about.

Interruption Advertising

For many generations across virtually every media, advertising sought to interrupt people's reading, listening, or viewing with a persuasive message. Over the last 25 years, the number of television channels and magazines exploded, allowing advertisers to select from more defined audiences. Targeting a medium toward a particular lifestyle or demographic allows advertisers to deliver more relevant messages. In this way, better targeted media led to more relevant creative.

The Internet took audience granularity to a whole new level. While many offline programs and publications were duplicated and even expanded upon in their online form, most online only publications are extremely specific in their target market. Media targeting leads to greater relevance to ads. This is critical at a time when consumers are bombarded by ads and in many cases are willing to pay money to avoid them (TiVo, Sirius, etc.).

The internet's greatest contribution to interruption advertising is derived relevance. Because the internet has ears, it can provide tools to shoppers that help them decide which features and benefits are most important to them. As the shopper's decision making moves forward, this derives relevance for advertisers.

If a shopping tool helps a shopper expand or contract their consideration set of products this opens up, or derives, an advertising opportunity of greater relevance than had previously existed. If a shopper suddenly discovers that Suzuki and Kia also make SUVs of the size the shopper was considering Honda, Toyota, Ford, and Chevrolet for, this creates a fantastic advertising opportunity for Suzuki or Kia. If the shopper determines that side-curtain airbags are a must have item for the SUV purchase, this derives a wonderful ad opportunity for an SUV manufacturer to highlight their side-curtain airbags and other safety features.

Services like Revenue Science make it possible to send many ads to the same person, once their online actions identify them to be a likely prospect. This is a good example of the internet's ears being used to better target interruption advertising to the right person multiple times.

One of the questions advertisers need to answer is whether frequency is more important than timing. Through behavioral advertising, someone who visited an automotive site and considered a full-size truck can then be sent a multitude of related ads on various other sites. However, the shopper may only be thinking about her vehicle consideration set when she is actively shopping for a vehicle. Being in front of the shopper when she is making vehicle shopping decisions is clearly more advantageous than when she is emailing, searching, or visiting other sites for other reasons.

The adjacent graphic demonstrates the difference between mass advertising, behavioral targeting, and a shopping site in terms of derived relevance. An advertisement aimed at the masses, like an ad on the home page of Yahoo, reached a low percentage of in-market shoppers for most goods. Behavioral targeting yields a very high percentage of shoppers who are in market now, yet these shoppers were intercepted some place where the context of the content is very different from the purpose of the product. Therefore, the audience was not thinking about the product category at the time they were intercepted.

Derived Relevance Improves Targeting and Timing

When the audience is intercepted on a shopping site related to that product category (e.g. a motorcycle ad on Cycletrader.com) they are both in market and thinking about the product category now. No one goes to Cycletrader.com looking for a donut. In 2008 I coined the term "when relevance" to describe this higher form of audience relevance. The ad is coming at the exact time they are shopping for the product category. Getting the right audience is "who relevance." Getting them at the moment they are thinking about the product category is "when relevance."

Large retailers representing a multitude of competing brands extract shelving allowances and other promotional fees from manufacturers. Many shoppers still make their purchase decisions within the store, making the retail store not only the distribution point for the product, but also a coveted place for promotions. A great deal of creativity has gone into in-store promotions. End of aisle displays can be extremely valuable real estate. Even promotional statements on the store floor and shopping carts can be powerful promotional space, particularly for new product launches.

Retailer ads are also an important place for manufacturers to promote their goods. Co-op advertising, the practice of manufacturers paying for the portion of a retailer's ad that promotes the manufacturer's product, is well established and now runs in the billions of dollars.

Whether a retailer's website is viewed as a promotional tool or an extension of the retailer's store, there is clearly an opportunity for retailers to offer promotional opportunities to manufacturers. These promotional opportunities are as carefully targeted as anything in the store. A manufacturer of welding equipment can have their ad seen exclusively by shoppers in the market for welding equipment at the exact time they are gathering product information and making shopping decisions in this specific category.

When retailers represent competing products, they have an opportunity to play the role of trusted advisor to the consumer, rather than just a product representative for the manufacturer. The same is true online. Retailers can provide shopping tools that help shoppers find the right product or combination of products to meet the shoppers' needs.

Direct Marketing

If radio and television ads are interruption advertising, then many forms of direct mail, telemarketing, email, and door-to-door are all interruption sales processes. The objective is to instantly originate demand and cause a specific action toward a purchase. In some cases, the entire sales process, through delivery, happens on the spot.

The marketer may target shoppers or canvas an entire community of people. Indeed, when I sold door-to-door in Southern California, we called it canvassing. One or more car loads of us would cover a neighborhood. There was very little targeting other than the selection of the neighborhood. The practice is still used today for political campaigning in tight elections.

More targeted forms of direct marketing are the basis for many multi-level marketing programs. In theory, you know your friends, neighbors and family members well enough to know who needs the product and who does not.

The term "direct marketing" carries many negative connotations.[10] However, there are times when a marketer feels certain a consumer should be interested in their product even if they are not. Direct marketing is very measurable. If it doesn't pan out financially, it does not continue.

---

[10] I carry some of the responsibility for these negative connotations. Years ago I participated in virtually every known form of direct marketing, generating direct impressions by the tens of thousands. In the process, I enhanced quality of life for a few people and bothered many more. As targeting improves, direct marketing may regain some sense of honor among those who disparage it. My stance remains the same as it did over 30 years ago: if you have reason to believe someone's life would be better after purchasing your product, giving them an opportunity to buy is nicer than keeping it a secret.

Chapter 13

Sales Network

Search Engines

Many of us conduct dozens of searches each day. When a question pops into our minds, we can instantly search for an answer. The ability to scan a huge portion of the world's information and instantly receive that which is relevant provides independence for problem solving. This includes solutions requiring the acquisition of a product or service.

Centuries of shopping history fell by the wayside with the advent of search engines. Historically, socialization played a huge role in the exchange of solutions information. Prior to the first really good search engines coming of age (circa 1999), shoppers were extremely dependent upon socialization and interruption advertising for market information. This system was inefficient and incapable of supporting consumers in an age of rapid change and product proliferation.

Far more of the buzz on social media sites would be about product related solutions, were it not for the independence granted by search engines. In many cases, demand origination begins with no more than a problem definable by a few keywords. Putting those key words into a search engine can introduce a range of solutions for sale or solutions involving acquirable components.

Much has been said and written about search engines being the first site shoppers access in so many shopping processes. That is not search engines' greatest contribution to sales integration. It is the fact that shoppers know they can abandon their current shopping process at any time and identify a new starting point through a search engine. The shopper's exit barriers are reduced when they know they can quickly identify an alternative solution.

It doesn't matter if you are the only shop in town selling floor lamps, the shopper can buy them online. It doesn't matter if your website is called Floorlamps.com, the shopper can find another site. Search engines don't just provide suggested places for solutions; they provide alternative solutions to problems. Not only are consumers independent in their ability to obtain market information, they can obtain lots of market information from alternative sources.

Each touchpoint covered in the upcoming chapters of this book is more sensitive because search engines make it so easy for shoppers to alter their course. No matter where a shopper is online, one or more search engines are always a single click away. Why are bounce rates so high? Because the back button sends shoppers right back to the search engine page showing all your competitors. Your landing page had better be ready to start selling a solution to the shopper's problem.

Imagine trying to sell someone something, knowing he only needs to touch a button to turn you off and quickly find another salesperson to work with. That is exactly what happens online. It will increasingly happen in stores as well. For many consumers, having an internet-enabled smartphone in their pocket gives them a license to call B.S. on any salesperson at any time.

Smartphones give shoppers access to information and alternatives. Yes, they may have to start over with another salesperson somewhere else, but they know where they are going and why they favor that alternative. Search engines lower exit barriers for shoppers in the sales process. Smartphones make it possible to lower those exit barriers any time, any place.

Product Search and Comparative Shopping Engines

One of the most exciting areas impacting the way consumers shop is the range of services posting product and price comparisons available from a variety of retailers. Comparative Shopping Engines (CSEs) like PriceGrabber.com and Shopping.com match product requests to posted prices from various retailers. Price is not the only consideration, so retailer ratings are provided as well.

I will not weigh in on a formal definition for what is and is not a CSE. From a consumer perspective, Bing Shopping and Google Product Search provide similar services. These sites are effective for rounding up a consideration set of products or a consideration set of retailers for a specific product.

As with the retailers themselves, there is room for improvement in product demonstrations. Retailers will need to look at their landing pages as well. Most are the same pages shoppers look at when they are choosing products from that retailer. A shopper coming from a CSE may not have the same information needs and probably does not have the same attachment to the retailer as a visitor coming to the retail site organically.

Common sense says someone trying to decide which retailer to buy the product from is going to have different information needs than someone organically on the retailer's site trying to decide which product to buy from that retailer. How best to facilitate the needs of all shoppers in a cost effective manner is a discussion that may last for many years. Nonetheless, efforts must be made and results measured.

With respect to sales integration, we must recognize CSEs are not just a source of site traffic. Shoppers are learning things about the mix of products, sellers, and market pricing on CSEs.

71

These impacts cannot be ignored. There is very real listening, matchmaking, and demonstrating going on. Although these sites do not sell a thing, they are undoubtedly a critical part of the sales process.

Information Sites

It is possible today to earn a decent living providing advice to shoppers, monetized by adjacent, relevant advertising. Thousands of online publications do just that. Many have complete autonomy from their advertisers, allowing Google or some other service to sell ad space on the site.

Shoppers may link to other sites found in the content of an information site. They may pick up key words on the information site, allowing them to refine their search. In some cases, they may obtain sufficient knowledge from the information site to abandon their online shopping and contact one or more stores. There is no universal path from an information site to a purchase.

By definition, shoppers cannot purchase from an information site, therefore information sites are often overlooked when designing distribution channels, but are essential to many multichannel shoppers. Working with information sites can range from advertising on them, to contributing content.

In some cases, companies choose to own their own information site. This can backfire on a brand if every article is just a puff piece. Worse still is when the site is used to attack competitors. Providing information about how to get the most from the product may be better received than simply information as to why your product is best.

Creating content that enhances consumers' quality of life will lead to more short-term sales, increased loyalty, and greater advocacy. Content can be placed on the store site or manufacturer site, but it can also often be delivered on information sites. If information sites are important to your shoppers, working cooperatively with these sites can play an important role in your sales integration strategy.

Directory Sites

Directory sites play an important role in service industries, where brand names are often weak and shoppers rarely shop for the category. Healthcare is a case in point. Healthgrades.com provides directories for nursing care, dental care, hospitals, doctors, and drugs. The shopper not only receives a list of facilities within the geographic area searched, but valuable information on how each nursing care facility rated in state inspections or what specialties each dentist has.

Properly done, directory sites can be more beneficial than search engines for getting the shopper to the right company. Directory sites often offer very relevant advertising opportunities.

At a minimum each company must monitor the information provided by these sites and the comments made about that company and its competitors. Good advertising in the right place at the right time may win a company more than its share of traffic from the website.

Some websites require payment for having your company listed on the site. Some list every vendor for free and charge a premium for the privilege of having an advanced listing. The key metric is the number of contacts. The number of phone calls can only be tracked properly if a dedicated number is assigned to the advertisement. The number of emails and chats need to be tracked with 100% accuracy. Walk-in traffic generated from the ad must be estimated. For businesses with very little walk-in traffic, like medical services, this is not a problem. For businesses with constant walk-in traffic, like florists, the amount of walk-in traffic attributable to the service must be estimated to assure the service is not discontinued bases on an incorrect performance measurement.

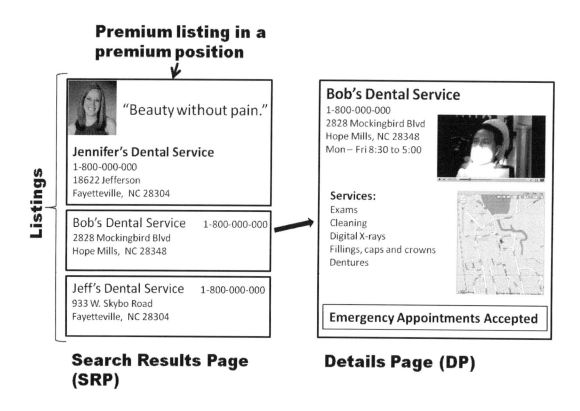

Premium listing in a premium position

"Beauty without pain."

Jennifer's Dental Service
1-800-000-000
18622 Jefferson
Fayetteville, NC 28304

Bob's Dental Service   1-800-000-000
2828 Mockingbird Blvd
Hope Mills, NC 28348

Jeff's Dental Service   1-800-000-000
933 W. Skybo Road
Fayetteville, NC 28304

Listings

Bob's Dental Service
1-800-000-000
2828 Mockingbird Blvd
Hope Mills, NC 28348
Mon – Fri 8:30 to 5:00

Services:
Exams
Cleaning
Digital X-rays
Fillings, caps and crowns
Dentures

Emergency Appointments Accepted

Search Results Page (SRP)   **Details Page (DP)**

Some models provide sufficient information in the listings themselves for the shopper to make a decision about which merchant to contact. For these models, conversion rate to a Details Page is not as important as total number of contacts divided by the number of exposures on Search Result Pages. Models requiring the shopper to go to the details page for contact information need to be measured in their conversion from Search Results Page to Details Page.

In addition to quantity, the quality of the contacts received must be considered. Generally speaking, the more information the site provides about vendor choices, the further the shopper can go in the sales process, and the more ready to buy he will be when he calls.

The value of a listing varies greatly by region. If the website has low penetration of providers, it may not be able to make a market. A search on 1800Dentist.com produced 53 dentists for 90503 in Torrance, CA. The same search for 28348 in Hope Mills, NC produced no results. This may appear to be a blockbuster opportunity for any dentist in the Hope Mills area, but a single vendor result will not inspire confidence in a shopper looking to compare dentists.

A consumer calling one of the 53 dentists listed in the Torrance area is probably a high quality contact. They had 53 to choose from and they are calling you! Of course, those other 52 remain just a click away, so it is important to handle the inquiry in the best possible way. The person answering the phone should be extremely familiar with content in the About Our Office section related to their practice.

This page should be continuously open on her computer for reference.

Content on the site will play a key role in the percentage of shoppers selecting your business. Staying with our example on 1800Dentist.com, 17 of the 53 dentist offices listed in the Torrance area did not have a photo on their listing. The dentist's portrait is the first thing that stands out on the listings, and the lack of a photo will hurt the rate at which the site produces contacts.

The value of a premium listing should be judged by the marginal improvement in contacts or the number of times your location or website is selected. Sometimes a premium listing simply stands out from the pack, sometimes it provides more information, and sometimes premium means premium placement.

FindAFlorist.com places member florists ahead of non-members in the listings and shows them in a superior listing format. Premium members are included in the adjacent map with listings at the top of the premium section.

FarmersMarket.com is a national directory of farmers' markets. Listing a farmer's market is free, to assure coverage in as many communities as possible. Gold membership expands the amount of information included in the listing. This model makes sense for industries with few merchants, or in this case, few markets within the average shopping radius. For industries with lots of competing merchants, like dental and floral, this model would not generate as much revenue as one that offers pay for placement and enhancement of directory listings.

IndieBound.org provides an interesting community model. Members can add a store at any time. There are no fees for listing a store and no premium listings. The site is provided by the American Booksellers Association, the national trade association for independent booksellers. The site is also useful for locating independent coffee shops, bike shops, toy stores, and other independent retailers.

The addition of other independent businesses in the search tool increases loyalty to independent bookstores. The site fosters an almost cult like passion for buying from independent retailers in general. There are a number of sites attempting to do the same for Hispanic or African-American businesses, but no national sites have achieved a sufficient number of listings to make a market.

Listing Sites

Listings Sites are like directories at the inventory level. The broad category of listing sites includes those populated by inventory feeds and those fed by scraping data from the internet. It includes unit listings, like a red 1967 Chevrolet Impala found on AutoTrader.com. It also includes new units, some of which may be unique and some with identical products offered through the same store or others.

Each month, millions of shoppers visit AutoTrader.com and Cars.com to choose among the vehicles. A comparatively few search by dealer. The dealer directory on these automotive inventory-listing sites is generally thrown in as an added value. Some sites do not include dealers in the directory unless they list their inventory on the site. Cars.com views the directory as a consumer service and includes as many known dealers as possible with an enhanced listing for those dealers posting their inventory on the site.

Listings were common for used durable goods long before the internet came of age. Listings in newspapers and printed shoppers remain an important consideration today. However, there is far less to manage in print publications because there is less that can be said about each product. It will never be cost effective to provide the level of product information in print that can be displayed online.

The two most important pages related to online listings are the Search Results Page (SRP) and the Details Page (DP)[11]. The example below is an example of the SRP and DP for new trucks. The SRP lists all the relevant products within the shopper's search criteria. Often, the SRP shows the shopper how many products meet their criteria and allows the shopper to refine their search.

Search Results Page (SRP)

---

[11] The automotive industry refers to these as Vehicle Details Pages (VDPs). The generic term is best for our purposes, since the other products, (i.e. stationary equipment and farm implements) are sold via listings as well.

Details Page (DP)

From the SRP, the shopper can click on any listing for more details, the DP. Site real estate is scarce on the SRP, giving the shopper just enough information to decide which products to investigate further. In most cases, shoppers do not contact retailers directly from the SRP.

Some shoppers contact the first retailer associated with the first DP they select. Others will spend hours forming a consideration set of products by clicking into multiple DPs and weighing the overall attractiveness of each one. In other words, not every click onto a DP is of equal weight. Some are from shoppers who pick from the SRP and some are from shoppers who explore from the SRP. It is important to measure conversion rates on this page. How many SRPs are you receiving per listing per shopper? How many DP are you receiving per SRP?

Maximizing the number of SRPs per listing per shopper is a function of having the right product and knowing how to work within each site's display model. How are products listed for the shopper? What percentage of listings is on the first SRP displayed? Is it sorted by price or some other attribute? Can you buy your way to the top of the list?

The number of SRPs received for each listing depends somewhat on the popularity of that listing. More shoppers search for a Honda Accord than for a Range Rover, yet most sites aggregating listings show only a limited number on each page. If the shopper looks at all of the pages showing

77

Accords, then each listing shows up on a SRP, still some shoppers do not search through hundreds of listings.

This is why sites aggregating listings are a different value proposition in large markets than they are in small markets. In a small market, there may only be 50 Accords available, so every vehicle listed shows up on a SRP every time a search is made for that model. In a larger market, there may be 500 Accords. The number of SRPs per vehicle per visitor will be lower in the larger market than in the smaller market. This is largely mitigated by the fact the site has more visitors in the larger market. However, the marketer must know how each listings site operates in each relevant market and how to get the most out of each system.

Cars.com lists vehicles by price, with the most expensive vehicles showing up on top. Most shoppers either reverse this order or use it to scroll down to the price level where they are comfortable. Expensive vehicles may receive many SRPs, but that does not count for much if they are so expensive shoppers skim right by them. Shoppers are savvy. What matters most is not where your product appears initially, it is where your product appears after the shopper's initial sorting of the inventory. There is need in the industry for a new metric, Post-Sort SRP. This would negate those SRP impressions that appeared initially, but were immediately sorted out.

Accords show up in more SRPs than Range Rovers do because there are a lot more people looking for them, and there are usually more Accords listed than there are Range Rovers.

For many industries, this is the marketplace. If your product is not listed on the website, you have no chance to get a SRP. Some listings sites dominate various categories. I hear consultants tell auto dealers collectively, "If you didn't give AutoTrader.com your inventory people would stop going to their website." The reality for any individual store is once you stop putting your inventory on AutoTrader.com, you will immediately experience a decrease in phone calls, emails, chats, and walk-in customers.

Sites like AutoTrader.com and Cars.com are effective marketplaces. Shoppers know they can find selection there. Sellers know shoppers go there. It may be important for retailers or manufacturers to list their products on a multitude of listings sites. Most of the inventory on Cars.com can also be found on AutoTrader.com; however, most of the Cars.com site visitors do not visit AutoTrader.com. What is true for automobiles also applies to motorcycles, boats, agricultural equipment, and a wide range of other products listed on independent websites.

The Economics of Aggregator Models

In industries where products must be aggregated from a variety of retailers in order to make a sufficient market for the consumer, the optimal place to operate is as an aggregator. The key success factor as an aggregator is getting sufficient inventory and getting retailers to pay to be there. This pay-to-play model is extremely difficult to establish. The aggregator must sign enough merchants to provide sufficient inventory to satisfy shoppers' needs. It is like rolling a train. Once it is rolling, it is not difficult to keep it rolling or even increase the speed. The trick is in getting the train to start rolling in the first place. Once a site is big enough to make a market, it can get bigger yet.

Within the automotive industry, the Vast model scrapes inventory and lists it free. Partner websites expose those listings to shoppers. The partner websites then try to sell premium listings or premium placement to dealers who want additional store traffic. This model of combining free and premium listings is common across many industries.

It will be years before a pay-to-play model takes hold in the elder care industries, like assisted living and nursing care. Some facilities only have a few vacancies, and some may even have waiting lists. Facilities in this industry do not typically post their vacant inventory on their websites, so there is no inventory database to easily post online. In contrast to the apartment and hotel industries, the facility is the listing, not the inventory within the facility.

If a community has only three assisted living facilities, the aggregator must have all three to sufficiently make a market for consumers. Contrast this with automobiles. The largest 20% of dealers control well over half the inventory in a community, and half of the community's inventory is nearly always sufficient to make a good shopping experience.

Compounding the difference between these two industries is the impact of the internet on the radius in which shoppers are willing to shop. Because shoppers can learn a great deal about a vehicle online, the radius is expanding for most auto shoppers. It would probably not be worth traveling 50 miles to check a dealer's prices and inventory. When shoppers are certain the right vehicle at the right price is at a store 50 miles away, they often make the trip. The default radius for Cars.com is 30 miles. For AutoTrader.com, it is 25 miles. Over 80% of shoppers living in rural communities change the shopping radius on these search sites to 100 miles or more.

A bigger shopping radius means a lower percentage of the total dealer universe is necessary to make a sufficient market for all shoppers in that universe. A shopping radius of 25 miles covers 1,963 square miles. A shopping radius of 50 miles covers 7,850 square miles. A doubling of the radius quadruples the shopping area, and in many cases quadruples the number of dealers and the amount of inventory.

With elder care, the shopping radius is primarily dictated by the desirability of the location, including ease of visitation. The ability to obtain information online has very little impact on the shopping radius. Most elder care sites are not very informative, but even if that changes it will not have a substantial impact on where shoppers are willing to shop. The problems of aggregation are not expected to ease in the short run.

The same is true in the plumbing business, except the radius is constrained from the supply side. Most shoppers never really cared where their plumber came from, so long as their drain got fixed in a timely manner and as cheap as possible. The radius has always been constrained by the cost of travel for the plumber, and nothing about online shopping will change that. The penetration necessary for an aggregator to be able to use a pay-to-play model is not going to change.

Prior to the internet, yellow pages became a huge success using a pay-to-play model that began with an extremely low entry point. This worked because the companies selling yellow pages had huge sales teams that only had to come to town once per publication. The fact that listings could not be added or removed helped with the penetration effort. It left some listings up longer than the companies lasted, but that was better than not having enough good listings to make a market.

The Yellow-Pages model came online, in a number of forms. Category sites offer wonderfully detailed information. The database fields that apply to one industry do not work at all for another, so sites aggregating a variety of industries are constrained in their ability to deliver automated models. Sites focused on a single category, or a limited range of categories, can bring far more utility to the shopping process than sites covering every business under the stars. On the other hand, sales efforts are less cost effective for category specific sites.

Combining Industries Results in Fewer Information Fields in Listings

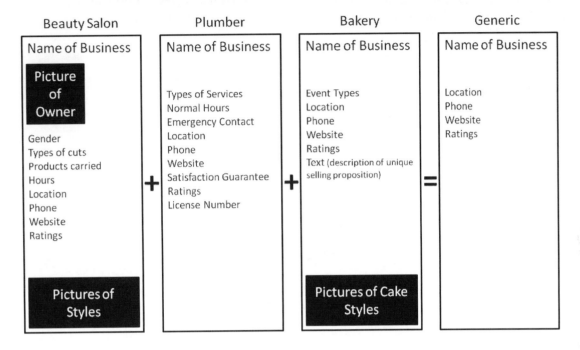

Publishers know the big money comes from face-to-face sales. Phone sales just do not bring in the same revenue per customer as in-person selling. Of course, it is much more cost effective to call on every retailer in town than it is to call on every pest control company. Additionally, everyone knew about yellow pages. That is not the case for web publishers. Every month, millions of auto shoppers visit Cars.com to see the inventory posted by more than 15,000 dealers. Yet I still run into used-car dealers who do not know the first thing about Cars.com. Penetration among sellers is a challenge for online shopping sites, regardless of the opening price.

Anyone with enough cash can enter a category at any time with a model that posts information about every business in the category. The money from this model comes from premium listings with additional information, and/or premium placement, and/or banner advertising. The variety of approaches delivers varying impacts on shopper satisfaction.

With banner adverting as the only revenue stream, the sellers are not involved and the listings do not improve in quality. By selling the ability to add photos, video, and text descriptions, the publication becomes a better user experience with every sale.

Publishers cannot sell premium placement to everyone. The model below is entirely theoretical. There are points on the graph that will never be empirically tested, and those using a premium placement model are in no rush to have me test these hypotheses. Nonetheless, there is merit to the discussion. I have participated in debates on this subject with hundreds of millions of dollars in revenue hanging in the balance.

Premium Positioning Model Tradeoff
Impact of Penetration on Stakeholder Satisfaction

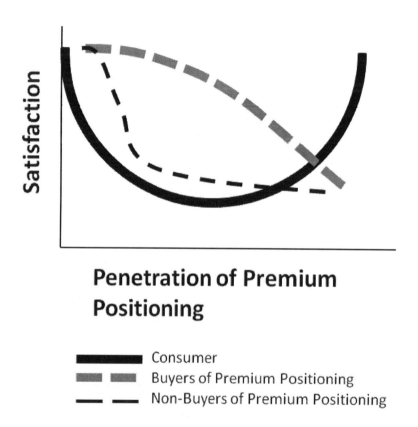

As a higher percentage of vendors buy the premium positioning, the problem gets worse and worse for consumers until over half of the inventory is premium. After that, the premium section becomes more and more the section for listings. At the point where all listings have premium positioning, the shopper experience is the same as it was with no premium positioned listings.

When premium positioning is sold, the more retailers added to the premium program the less each one benefits from the program. There is a tipping point here when industry discussion starts buzzing about the fact that if everyone pays to gain an advantage then no one receives it. As is often seen in game theory, it is very difficult for competitors to collude, even when it is in their mutual best interest to do so. However, there is a point where talk of a revolt heats up and begins to impact the website's reputation and long-term growth potential among retailers.

Those vendors not participating in premium positioning find their listings pushed further and further into the back as penetration grows. There is a point where the incremental impact is minimal. For those detailed searches yielding only enough listings for one page, the movement of a few spaces on the page has little impact on the number of contacts. For those searches yielding multiple pages of search results, those consumers who understand the need to hunt past the premium listings for bargain prices will do so regardless of the depth in premium listings.

Since those managing the site have no real sense of how far is too far until they reach it, this is a tricky model to manage. It is an impossible model to manage without market leadership and company leaders who stay extremely close to their retailers.

Leads Models

One way to monetize a shopping site is to turn shoppers into leads, which are then sold to participating companies operating within that category. Leads reverse the flow of communications. The vendor purchasing the lead is required to contact the shopper. However, shoppers are not obligated to halt their shopping process to wait for a response.

Leads models peaked in some industries and are still going strong in others. Increasingly, independent sites recognize the need to add value with shopping information and tools. Just putting a lead form on the home page is not going to deliver much beyond a high bounce rate.[12]

Leads models flourish best in industries with long shopping cycles, multiple product variations, and with no strong aggregation models. A leads model is no good for emergency plumbing services, but it works fine for plumbing construction. When the shopper needs help fast, they want to stay in control of the communications. When they want to talk their needs over with an expert who can guide them into the right purchase, then waiting for a call or email from the right expert is generally okay.

There are two distinct kinds of leads. Blind leads offer the shopper no choice in which vendor will call on them. Increasingly, leads models are providing choice and transparency to the shopper by disclosing the vendors available and offering the shopper a choice of which vendors the lead should go. As the internet becomes better at facilitating self-help, blind leads models will decline.

---

[12] Wikipedia: "Bounce rate essentially represents the percentage of initial visitors to a site who 'bounce' away to a different site, rather than continue on to other pages within the same site."

Blind Lead

2010 Chrysler Town and Country Limited
Zip Code: 28348
MSRP: $35,060
Invoice Price: $33,039

First Name: [   ]

Last Name: [   ]

Phone Number: [   ]

E-mail Address: [   ]

Submit for Dealer Quote

Choice of Dealers

2010 Chrysler Town and Country Limited
Zip Code: 28348
MSRP: $35,060
Invoice Price: $33,039

First Name: [   ]

Last Name: [   ]

Phone Number: [   ]

E-mail Address: [   ]

Select up to 2 dealers:

☒ Neuwirth Motors   Accredited Dealer

☐ Hendrick Chrysler Jeep

Franchise and Group Sites

Independent sites are not the only ones forming aggregation models. Franchise and dealer group networks are claiming some of the same SEO and economy of scope benefits for the exclusive benefit of their affiliated stores.

It is very difficult for any independent auto repair shop to compete with Midas.com in SEO position or the quality and quantity of shopping content. Midas franchises its store outlets, and the objective of Midas.com is to send ready-to-buy traffic to those stores. It is much more cost effective to maintain one optimized site serving hundreds of stores than it is for each store to take on this challenge. . Indeed few shop owners are marketing experts. This service is a major attraction to franchising.

With television advertising, franchises benefit from buying regional or national spots at a lower cost per thousand (CPM). Economies of scope in advertising are one of the things that make franchising so popular. With online presence, the franchise advantage over independent stores is many times greater.

It is nearly impossible for any of Merle Norman's studios to have a website as comprehensive as MerleNorman.com. Many studios have their own websites, but they all benefit from the centralized marketing efforts of the franchisor.

Many Roto-Rooter franchises simply rely on their store page within RotoRooter.com. The franchisor does the selling up to the point of producing a phone call to the franchisee. This is how plumbers want to receive their business. Every service call is unique. A back and forth conversation over the phone between the consumer and a trained sales professional can better assure the plumber sent has the right parts and equipment to match the job; the match is demonstrated for the shopper, the deal is closed with understood terms, and the service delivery is to the right place at the right time.

Auto dealers are limited in their new-vehicle operation to what they are franchised to sell. Manufacturers provide websites that link to their franchised dealers' sites and their stores, but each manufacturer site is limited by the same constraint, they only show their products. Some dealer groups are designing sites that allow the shopper to compare the various vehicles sold by the dealer group across all of its stores. In this way, a group site delivers a similar benefit to consumers online as auto malls do offline.

Not all dealer groups take full advantage of their group site, or even have one. Some sites merely move the shopper to the appropriate store site. Manufacturers have some influence over this behavior. Some manufacturers do not want their vehicles shown alongside competing vehicles. Within the dealer group, some store managers do not want their products to be seen alongside the products of other stores. (Frankly, I cannot imagine working someplace where I had that little confidence in my product.)

For those shoppers looking for comparisons, not providing this opportunity can send them clicking off to another site altogether. Chatlee Boat & Marine is North Carolina's largest boat dealer, carrying 20 brands of boats and motors. Unfortunately, the shopper must look at each brand separately on the retailer's website. The boats are separated by type within each brand, but the brands cannot be aggregated together to compare one fishing boat to another, or one cruise boat to another. Chatlee's huge selection is a competitive advantage, but it fails to exploit that advantage during the sales process on its website.

In some cases, the guidelines of coop advertising programs prohibit the comingling of competing brands. This is built on longstanding traditions regarding print advertising. If one fully recognizes the shopper's supremacy in the sales process, however, these policies begin to look foolish. In many cases, the shopper is sitting in the comfort of their own home or office with complete control over the mouse and keyboard. If they want to compare products they will. Coop funds should be provided to facilitate these comparisons on the sites of retailers carrying the manufacturer's inventory. They should further be provided for content demonstrating the superiority of the manufacturer's inventory.

Marketers with the attitude their job is to expose the shopper to their product and try to keep them from seeing anything from competitors should be straightened out or sent to pasture. Marketers are no longer free to cram product down the shopper's throat, nor can they put blinders on the shopper.

Both franchise sites and group sites are aggregators. Generally, franchise sites aggregate the stores offering their services or the franchise's products across all the stores. Product aggregation may be necessary if some franchisees carry only a portion of the franchisor's offerings. Smaller dealers tend to argue that a shopper from their area should be exposed only to inventory from their store. After all, if they do not have something in stock they can order it for the customer or trade with a dealer who does have it.

Again, the problem with this logic is the shopper is in control. If she would prefer to contact a further store with the product in stock than a closer one without the desired product, then that is what she is going to do. Making it hard for her only invites the shopper to consider another brand altogether.

Group sites become necessary when the collection of stores within a dealer group offers greater selection and service to consumers than either the franchisor or a single store. This is common in the automobile industry, where many manufacturers still insist on dealers carrying their brand and their brand only. Shoppers are left with only two places to find independent comparisons; independent sites the manufacturer has no control over and dealer group sites. It would seem advantageous for manufacturers of superior goods to support comparisons on group sites.

The same auto manufacturers complaining about dealerships carrying multiple brands within one store or displaying multiple brands on one website spend millions of dollars advertising on independent websites like kbb.com and Edmunds.com. These sites are extremely popular with consumers because they do provide unbiased side-by-side comparisons. Thousands of dealerships closed in recent years while independent websites grew to new heights.

Chain stores routinely provide group sites with store locators. The degree to which each chain's group site facilitates the sales process varies greatly. A chain of movie theaters may demonstrate the product and offer to close the sale. Others provide no greater service than to match the shopper with the nearest store.

Facilitating the entire sales process online may not be necessary, best, or even possible, however, the website must make it as easy as possible for the shopper to proceed confidently through the sales process. Holding back information and avoiding competitive comparisons are actions inconsistent with sales integration. Sales people do not avoid competitive comparisons; they welcome them. Sales people do not direct shoppers to the cash register; they facilitate the transaction. Site managers are part of a sales process and must be as cognizant of this responsibility as they are other forms of site usability.

Manufacturer Sites and Content

Influenced by loyalty, advocacy, or brand image, many shoppers begin their shopping process at a manufacturer's website. The homepage of the manufacturer's site must provide great navigation and site search capability, listening to where the shoppers are in their shopping process and to any questions they may have. Matchmaking capabilities generally need to be prominent on the home page. The obvious question on many manufacturer sites is "what category" or "what model." In some cases, it is "what lifestyle." If your site needs an answer to these questions in order to match the shopper with the right product, then your website needs to facilitate these decisions.

When I ran the automotive internet practice at J.D. Power and Associates, we provided the Manufacturer Website Evaluation Study to nearly every manufacturer serving the United States. Each time a manufacturer came up with a superior method of facilitating the model decision from the home page, their usefulness score improved. In 2003, many sites simply provided a list of models and asked the shopper to pick one. By 2006, virtually every manufacturer provided pictures of the vehicle along with pricing on the home page. The shopper did not need to remember which Ford SUV was the smaller, cheaper one. Information about the Escape and Explorer was immediately available on the home page to facilitate the model selection.

Once the match is made, the manufacturer must demonstrate value. Product quality, reliability, and durability are attributes most manufacturers are better capable of demonstrating than are their retailers. Their authority regarding the design, materials, and assembly contributing to these attributes ranks second to none.

Many companies achieve quality standards far in excess of that produced in the past. Yet perceptions of product quality are what move the revenue needle. Word of mouth about product quality changes can take many years to catch up with actual quality changes.

By definition, durable goods last more than one year; therefore, they are infrequently purchased. It takes much longer to change quality perceptions regarding dishwashers and vacuum cleaners than it does paper towels and trash bags.

The chart below highlights one consumer's shopping habits. It demonstrates how vastly different the marketing challenge is for marketers of durable goods compared to packaged goods. If we are going to judge a brand, we should have a sufficient sample size of the same product to make sure our perception is not just based on a product quality outlier. Most experts who study product quality insist on a sample size of at least 30 consumer experiences, and want more than 100.

Products	Purchase Frequency	Number of brands with 30 or more samples lifetime
Hamburgers	50 per year	3
Motorcycles	6 per lifetime	0
Breakfast Cereal	30 boxes per year	15
Automobiles	15 per lifetime	0
Hand Soap	18 per year	3
Computer	19 lifetime	0

With respect to some packaged goods, individual consumers get 30 samples or more each year. Packaged goods are also advantaged by the fact they do not change much over time. You cannot say that about most durable goods. Consumers do not get many product trials, and the product often changes between purchases.

Today, many durable goods are loaded with so many features that many of them go completely unnoticed during the entire life of the product. Auto dealers are often amazed by how many consumers trade in their vehicle without knowing how to use some of the features. The same could be said for many computers, video cameras, and telephones.

The phones I used for the first half of my life did only two things, dial outbound calls and ring when a call came in. No taking photos, no call waiting, no saving phone numbers, no telling me who is calling, and darn sure no internet. It was easy to measure the quality of a phone because it was just a phone. My phone today does so many things I do not know when it is broken and when I am just using it incorrectly.

With so many features and so few product purchases, is it really fair of any consumer to have an opinion of a durable goods brand? Well, life is not fair. Many consumers are going to have an opinion of product quality, and many of them are going to be very loud about their opinions, good and bad. Durable goods marketers are operating at a point in time when it is harder than ever for consumers to give an accurate assessment of product quality, yet they voice their opinions with the loudest megaphone in the history of the world, the internet.

Consumers also differ in their definition of product quality. Some think primarily of initial product quality; was it right coming out of the box? J.D. Power and Associates documented fantastic improvements in the automobile industry's initial product quality. Even the worst brands are better than the best brands were when the firm started tracking problems per 100 vehicles decades ago.

Some consumers think of reliability; does it do what it is supposed to do every time? This is an area where durable goods improved dramatically. Anyone who ever drove a vehicle built prior to the 1970s can probably remember a time when he could not get his car started. They flooded easily, among other problems. When was the last time you heard of a modern vehicle flooding? Who in the heck carries starter fluid in the trunk these days?

Products associated with wired or wireless services have a different challenge because very reliable hard goods are married with unreliable phone, cable, GPS, DSL, or other services. The reverse may also be true in some cases.

Some consumers focus on durability. In many cases, the first thing a consumer thinks about before he buys a durable good is how long the previous one lasted. Some durable goods undergo repairs and maintenance during their lifetime. The perception of their product durability will be impacted by the quality of repairs and service. Anything with an internal combustion engine fits this category.

Other durable goods are infrequently or never repaired or serviced during their lifetime. Durability may be measured by the amount of usage consumed prior to poor performance or it may simply be the amount of usage prior to failure. Many household appliances simply go until they stop. Today, many televisions, vacuum cleaners, and personal computers are discarded at first failure. Repair was once a common occurrence for these product categories, now it is rarely considered.

Most durable goods improved in product quality to a greater extent than consumer perceptions give them credit. Roughly half the brands in the automobile business have a higher perceived product quality gap relative to the market leaders than their actual product quality gap. Some brands provide better product quality than competitors who are less frequently avoided because of product quality perceptions. J.D. Power and Associates asks vehicle purchasers why they did not buy a similar product offered by another brand. The product quality of the brand is frequently mentioned. Hyundai had dramatic improvements in product quality and sustained that high quality for many years, yet the brand is still more frequently avoided based on product quality than other brands with inferior quality.

Product quality means different things to different people. Their perceptions of product quality are probably not based on anything like a scientific standard. This should make it easier to understand why marketers of durable goods must demonstrate product quality. If shoppers are going to think it, but they cannot experience it, then marketers must demonstrate it.

Actual product quality is largely a function of engineering, components, and production process. Since 2005, I called for online demonstrations of superior engineering, components, and processes in the automobile industry. Sadly, far too little has been done.

If ever a brand needed to demonstrate product quality it is Maytag. For years, the Maytag name was synonymous with quality, and then it all fell apart. Maytag is not going to get back its old customers or its premium margins unless it demonstrates its products improved, yet there is very little on their website that speaks to this. The shopper can "look inside a Maytag" (Home > Products > Laundry > Look Inside the Performance Series Washer by Maytag) and find the washer belt is the widest in the industry and has eight grooves to prevent slippage. That is great for the slippage issue, but how long before it breaks? Are there any special designs or compounds that extend belt life?

Maytag is thrilled to tell me that their ¾ horsepower motor will go 1,000 RPM, but I have no idea why I should care. How long will it last? Are the tolerances tighter to assure a longer lasting motor? Is it engineered to run cooler for longer wear? Is there some miracle graphite that reduces friction? Why in the world should consumers believe that Maytag quality once again lives up to the Maytag name?

Harley-Davidson has a brand image that most marketers and sales people would love to work with, but its reputation for quality suffers. One might think they would demonstrate their improved product on their website, especially with respect to touring bikes. Touring bikes are made for long distance and many years of reliable use. Yet all Harley-Davidson could think to say about their newly designed frame's contribution to quality was, "The new frame has 50 percent fewer parts and 60 percent fewer welds, providing rigidity and more cargo capacity."

Are you kidding me? Fewer connections mean fewer possibilities of a disconnection. A more rigid frame means that everything bolted onto it less likely to come loose. Instead of eliminating shopper doubts about quality, Harley-Davidson focuses on performance, image, and cleavage on their website.

Some will say it is best to focus on the positive aspects of your product and not bring attention to the things for which your brand has a negative reputation. If a shopper bought into your brand image deep enough to ignore your poor reputation for quality, then you do not have much of a sales challenge in front of you. But what about those who do care? Shouldn't your shopping site be designed to meet the information needs of every shopper considering your product? You are likely to find your brand evangelists are extremely grateful to hear about your quality improvements, especially if they have been apologists for your poor quality in the past. This kind of information empowers brand evangelists and encourages advocacy.

DeWALT addressed the issue of durability head on with a video demonstration for their battery-powered drills. The video demonstration compared the shifting ring of the DeWALT to the Makita. It spoke to the difference in components and took advantage of the video's site, sound, and motion to demonstrate convincingly their shifting ring was more ridged than the competition.

Makita had no video, and no mention of durability. It offered the classic text description of their product as well as spec sheets on each product. I have no idea why I should care that the 18V ½" LXT Lithium-ion Hammer Driver-Drill Kit Model BHP451 has a Blows/Min (BPM) of 0-25,500 in the high range. This is exactly the kind of crud you get when marketers simply take the information engineers give them and barf it all over the shopper. Are you trying to sell the product or not? DeWALT puts far more effort into selling $200 drill motors than Makita does it most expensive generator.[13]

Briggs & Stratton's micro site, www.enginesmatter.com used a video under the Longer Life section of the Ride Engines tab. The video explained the importance of a well-designed lubrication system to engine durability. Then it went on to show all four of its lubrication systems and demonstrated the superiority of its pressure system. What Briggs & Stratton did not compare their engine to competitors' engines. They already had a great reputation for quality and their video implied their market leading position was a result of their legendary quality. But the video did much more; it tried to up-sell the shopper to their best motor.

If I were selling riding mowers, I would want every customer and every salesperson to see this video. The mowers with the best engines are the ones with the most goodies and the highest prices, and customers will be more apt to spend the extra money if they think the product is going to last longer. If I were a manufacturer of riding mowers, I would want this video on my site, in my dealer's stores, in every sales training program, and in front of every customer. Now how likely would I be to drop Briggs & Stratton and start putting cheaper engines in my mowers? I have no idea why companies like Snapper and Murray did not avail themselves of any of this for their mowers featuring Briggs & Stratton engines.

Whether you demonstrate superior components like DeWALT or superior engineering like Briggs & Stratton, the net result is a more confident consumer. Empowering consumers with product information related to quality, durability, and reliability not only helps them feel confident they are making the right choice; it helps them confidently engage a salesperson. Many consumers fear salespeople and worry that a salesperson could steer them in the wrong direction. Product

---

[13] This analysis was conducted in 2009. Makita now has a static page demonstrating both its advanced motor design and the premium-grader raw materials used.

knowledge may be the difference between a ready-to-buy shopper in a showroom and a would-have-been shopper still trying to get by with the product they have.

Automobile manufacturers have the largest advertising budgets of any durable goods manufacturers, yet very little effort is put into demonstrations of product quality, durability, or reliability. Ford did a good job demonstrating its F-150 pickup trucks. Across the range of auto manufacturer sites, there was precious little else that deserved even mentioning.

Versatility is a quality in which more and more durable goods stake their claim. Consumers often appreciate one product that can serve multiple needs. Wouldn't it be terrible if we had to have multiple washing machines for each type of fabric? Having a multitude of cycles to get garments clean in the way safest for each fabric is a huge benefit, and additional cycles are a selling feature.

Honda did a good job demonstrating the versatility of its Ridgeline pickup truck. Honda introduced the Ridgeline as an innovative truck design that offered far more interior storage capacity relative to its overall size. Honda recognized some items are best hauled in a weatherproof area that can be locked down, without losing the advantages of a pickup bed.

Demonstrations of versatility usually require video. If a product transforms from one purpose to another, then there is usually visual change associated with that transformation. Examples include seats reconfiguring in an SUV or a table into bed within an RV. The motion of video can be combined with the appropriate sounds and/or voice narration to provide the credible mood and the sellable claim. Trying to demonstrate versatility with still pictures and text seems silly today. Even a cheap video would often be better than no video.

Occasionally, animation is required. This is very often the case with safety features. Air bags are nearly always demonstrated with some type of illustration or animation. The transition from a safe situation to an unsafe situation, then to a protected state requires motion, like video. Showing an actual crash or potential injury invoking situation, however, is generally best left to animation.

Product demonstrations and comparisons need not be limited to websites and advertisements. Manufacturers should take a leadership role in making sure the effort on their websites continue on to other touchpoints. In many cases, only the manufacturer can provide the proper demonstration content. In-store demonstrations are all too rare and easier than ever. It strikes me as strange that Target can have an in-store display that demonstrates various CDs, and Toys can be packaged in a way that allows trial of interactive features, yet there are very few stores offering powerful demonstrations of durable goods via video or any other means.

I am not suggesting that showrooms should become interactive museums that foster a real understanding of the product and its advantages prior to purchase, but that image may be a more cost-effective sale plan than watching the customer walk out the door empty handed.

There is an old saying in sales, "The more you tell, the more you sell." That is nonsense. The shopper is in charge now, and the more they understand the more you will sell. Help the shopper understand which product is right for him and why it is the best choice, and do it in the way the shopper wants to consume information and get the most out of it.

In-store hardware can be used for multiple models and multiple model years. The changes and updates are simply downloaded. Videos and interactive content can be centrally produced by the manufacturer to insure consistency of the brand message and economically distributed to the stores.

Currently, franchisors often place multi-million dollar burdens on franchisee retailers to meet standards for exterior appearance with few standards for product demonstration capabilities within the store. Manufacturers must first generate great content, however, and then hardware demands can be made of stores.

Distributor Sites

Some distributor sites are limited to the retailers they serve and require a password to access content. That is not the case for Diamond Comic Distributors, Inc. They openly provide regular industry reports, like the top 100 comics. They publish market share for each of the publishers, by dollars and units. They provide a top 10 list of toys and statues based on comic book characters and a similar top-10 list of games. They sell these products to distributors along with comics.

Clearly, this information is designed for comic book retailers, both customers and potential customers. Given the depth of passion some fans have about their comic book characters, there is no doubt some consumers are accessing Diamondcomics.com as well. The site links to kidscomics.com, also owned by Diamond Comic Distributors.

KidsComics.com provides news and information to consumers as well as an extremely prominent retailer locator. This is an industry whose retailers tend to be very small, and can use all of the help they can get driving traffic into the store. The distributor engages consumers in order to help drive store traffic.

Golden Eagle Distributors, Inc. provides a site clearly designed for consumers and social activists, gedaz.com. The site provides information about events. Its "Show in Love" tab provides information about all of the socially responsible activities in which the organization participates. It also links to industry sites like beeresponsible.com, Anheuser Busch's corporate social responsibility website.

The site links to manufacturer sites for each of the beverages it distributes. This is a clear recognition of the distributor's understanding of the fact that shoppers do not always seek information in the same flow with which goods are distributed. Many of the merchants stocking Golden Eagle's beverages are small retailers, restaurants, and bars. Most of them are unable to put anything like this together.

For most of us, beer is not a big deal and what we drink does not define us, but the thirstiest 20% of beer drinkers consume most of the beer. Providing content to keep drinkers loyal and proud of their brands can be fantastic marketing. Golden Eagle Distributors could do more to encourage advocacy of the site, but this is an excellent step forward for a distributor participating in sales integration.

Physical Stores

For many products, it is no longer the case that most shoppers coming into the store begin the sales process there. The vast majority of shoppers for autos, RVs, trailers, motorcycles, boat, and many other goods begin the sales process online and then transition to the physical store. Treating these shoppers as though they do not know anything about your product or competing offerings is a prescription for disaster.

Selling to shoppers who already began their sales process online requires no additional skills, but the importance of listening skills is amplified. To sell effectively, the salesperson must understand what the shopper experienced online. Many shoppers are guarded about this information, particularly in situations where price is negotiable.

Noticing trigger words and phrases is important. If a truck shopper mentions he has kids in sports, the salesperson needs to think about the cargo net accessory that will safely store dirty, sweaty clothes and shoes without the need for putting them in the cab. This solves a problem while emphasizing the fine interior qualities of the new truck.

Is the shopper safety conscious? Will they need to tow anything? What cargo will they carry? Rather than a data dump of product facts, the salesperson must listen for needs and concerns and gently probe when necessary.

The salesperson must know what information is provided on sites carrying the product and competing products. This is where sales processes often break down. BestBuy.com is a wonderful website that is integrated with the inventory in Best Buy stores and warehouses. Some of the clerks working in the stores, however, are virtually useless. Integrating computer information systems can be difficult. Integrating information systems with human salespeople is extremely difficult.

Product proliferation makes it hard for many sales people to keep up with the stock they carry. Keeping up with competitive offerings can be extremely hard. This challenge is compounded by frequent employee turnover. In many cases, employees do not find the job rewarding because they are not able to add a great deal of value. Yet they cannot add a great deal of value unless they stick with it long enough to become product experts as well as professional listeners.

Retailers must provide their employees with more and better training in a cost-effective manner. Filling this need with live training is nearly impossible. The faster things change, the more time trainers must spend on keeping up with the changes and the more training employees need. In other words, the number of trainers needed increases with the pace of change at an almost exponential rate. Unless there is reason to think the pace of change in your industry is going to level off or slow down, consideration must be given to recorded means of training.

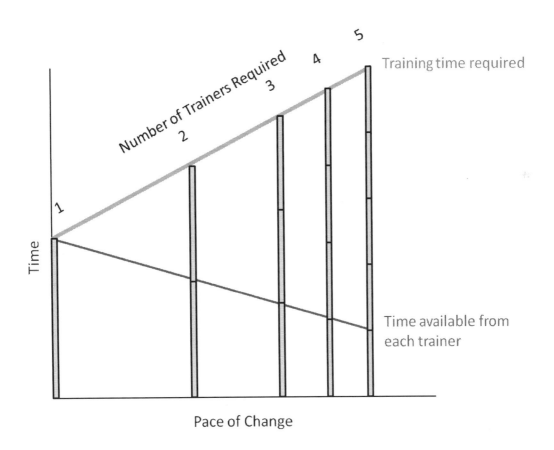

As mentioned previously, in-store kiosks are becoming more prevalent. Some stores even provide personal computers with internet connections for customer use. Kiosks and PCs are used for a variety of purposes:

1. Accessing inventory not available in the physical store
2. Product demonstrations that cannot be done in the store otherwise
3. Accessing accessory catalogs
4. Accessing online owner's manuals and warranty information
5. Providing credible documentation regarding finance rates, product alternatives, value demonstrations, etc.

Store personnel need to know what is online throughout the sales network. It is also important for them to know what information the shopper may need that the online sales process did not provide. Some rental car companies are notorious for taking online reservations without letting the shopper know a deposit, as well as the full transaction amount, will be withdrawn from their credit card at the time of purchase. Shoppers running their credit cards close to the limit are rejected at the counter without ever being notified during their online reservation process or their in-store delivery process of the full amount that would be withdrawn.

I witnessed a woman traveling with an infant making frantic calls for help in the middle of her travel in order to get the rental car she thought she had planned for so carefully. The agent at Advantage behaved like an indifferent guardian of corporate policy. As it turned out, not taking the insurance or prepaying the gas would have reduced the cost enough for her credit card to cover the rental and the deposit, but that was not the clerk's concern. He was not part of the sales process. It was not his job to help shoppers make transactions, and he certainly was not responsible for anything that occurred online. In his view, his job at Advantage was strictly limited to enforcing the rules.

One of the great tragedies of disintegration occurs when store personnel wash their hands of the internet, which occurs constantly. Store personnel feel no responsibility to know what messages are sent online, in fact many act as though the shopper is causing a problem at the physical store by referring to anything online. "Don't you know that is a different world I have nothing to do with? What time is my break anyway?" Fixing online integration problems requires identifying them, but fixing problems offline requires an acknowledgement that selling and sales integration are important in the first place.

Store Websites

The store website may sell the product, send the shopper to the physical store, send the shopper to a contact center, or any combination of the three. Some store sites represent only those products available in the store while others offer far more products than any retail store could ever stock. An example of the diversity of store sites is demonstrated in the chart below.

Distribution Model	Example	Common Reasons for Model Selection
All sales closed at store or with contact center	Auto, boat, and motorcycle dealers; restaurant; auto service; elder care	Product is a major purchase, service needs are difficult to assess
Sales closed at store or online, all non-custom products available through either channel	Bank, florist, bakery	Inventory is identical through all distribution channels. Product is often intangible, made to order or perishable
Sales closed at store or online, some products not available through all channels	Sears.com, BestBuy.com	Retail outlet cannot inventory all items

Regardless of whether or not the site is designed to close the sale, it must contribute to the sales process by listening, match making, and demonstrating.

If the site sends shoppers to a contact center, it should let the shopper know what can be expected from the contact center. Will there be an expert who can answer shopping questions or just an appointment maker?

Shoppers feel frustrated when they click on a link that does not provide what they expected from that link. The frustration can be much greater when linking to a human who cannot help in the manner expected. Some businesses feel any transition from online shopping to human contact is a step forward, but this is not always the case. Much of this misunderstanding originates with a failure to recognize that a good store site contributes to the sales process. Store sites are not just introductions to the store; they are an extension of it.

DollarGeneral.com has no shopping cart. Shoppers can find the specials, construct a shopping list, and print their list, but they must go to the physical store to make their purchases. The target market of Dollar General is households with less than $75,000 annual income in communities of over 4,500 people. As their target market becomes increasingly accustom to internet shopping, this strategy may need review. Currently, service is not the hub of this business model. Many consumers are willing to do a little work in order to receive the lowest prices possible. In fact, service options like curbside pickup could signal that prices are too high, even if the actual prices remain the same.

Dollar General is not practicing multiple channel marketing; they have one channel and one channel only. However, they are facilitating multichannel shopping. Some of their shoppers go straight to the store. Some of them wait for the print ads to arrive. Some of them go online to check the specials and see what is available. They all buy from the store; the paths they take to get there differ.

Contact Center

Many shoppers reach out to a contact center after being online. If the sales process has been going on at any number of websites linked to the contact center by phone, email, or chat, then it is essential for those working in the contact center to have these screens open prior to taking calls. Contact center personnel must be extremely familiar with the information available to shoppers prior to the call and be able to catch up as quickly as possible.

No matter where the shopper is in the sales process, the first step for contact center personnel is listening. Few things are more destructive to the sales process than assumptions about what the shopper wants.

In every industry, trigger words and phrases should ignite a probe for additional information. For automobiles, finding out the shopper is a cyclist triggers an introduction to bike racks. If the shopper uses a truck for work or for transportation to varying work sites, this triggers a discussion about work tools and options for keeping them safe and secure.

What things do consumers do with your product that triggers the need for options or accessories? What information might your sales network hear that would justify a probe into these needs? Does your website address these trigger words or phrases? What paths might the shopper have taken to meet these needs online? What alternatives does the shopper have to meet these needs?

If the contact center cannot close the sale, then it must set an appointment with someone who can. Contact centers should not refer customers back to the website if there is any other way of obtaining the sale. Shoppers know they can go to the website whenever they want to. They called for help, and that help should get them to a close if possible.

Auction Sites

EBay is the largest and best known auction site. The auction process is great for market transparency. Shoppers find sellers; sellers find a market for their product, and both find the intersection point of supply and demand.

Size matters with auction sites. The seller always receives the highest price available within the available auction audience at a given point in time. If the auction draws an insufficient audience, there is a smaller probability the price achieved would prove to be the highest available at that time if the audience included all in-market shoppers. This audience of all in-market shoppers is purely theoretical, but it remains an appropriate benchmark for audience comparisons, and no one comes closer to that benchmark than eBay.

Since a bid is a commitment, sellers must meet shoppers' information needs in order to attract competitive bids. Even if all in-market shoppers were exposed to the offer, the maximum price could only be achieved if all information needs were met. Uncertainty lowers transaction prices.

Auctions often take place among similar products at the same time. Consider tickets to a sporting event. In some sense, every reserved seat is a unique product. The face value for a given section is generally the same, however, and many ticket pairs provide equal value if all other variables are the same. The trick to receiving top dollar lies in providing more information about the tickets and the transaction process. If bidders have a choice between a pair of tickets with a stadium map link showing the location and a description of how wonderful the last event was from those seats, it would probably sell faster and/or for a higher price than an adjacent pair without supporting information.

The following list of merchandising tips can be found on listings from expert sellers:

1. No view obstructions (or if there is one, point out what can be seen)
2. Seating chart
3. Information about the event
4. Parking information
5. Why the tickets are available
6. Information about the sales process
    a. Payment options
    b. How the tickets will be delivered
    c. Background on the seller

All of this contributes to greater confidence in the ticket delivery and event satisfaction. Both factors can increase the final offer amount. Some shoppers will be more willing to bid and some will be willing to bid more than they otherwise would.

Raising both the number of bidders and the preference relative to other alternatives may not produce a premium in every case. A seller of a single pair of tickets may need to do a lot of work to improve the probability of a superior price. A seller with a multitude of tickets can develop a fairly automated method for merchandising tickets that will surely pay off over time.

The most misunderstood aspect of auction sites is the false sense that multichannel shopping does not apply. Shoppers go from auction sites to the seller's website to see what else they have to offer and at what price. They may visit the seller's website to gain confidence regarding delivery or find out about accessories. The shopper may visit the manufacturer's site to find additional product information. They may visit listings sites to identify alternatives. The seller must be cognizant of what information other sites provide. The seller may even wish to provide links to information sources providing additional credibility.

Some sellers view auction sites as self-service systems. This is not necessarily the case. Listening to the customer remains important in an auction situation. The seller must prepare for calls, chats, emails, and walk-in traffic from auction listings. As discussed previously, many shoppers buy something different once in the store than they intended to while online. Online auctions are not exempt from this. Some of these shoppers contact the seller about a vehicle they intend to bid on and buy a different vehicle instead. Even if the shopper bids on a product, it does not mean the match was perfect. The deal could unwind, and astute sellers prefer to replace weak matches with stronger ones within their own inventory.

Purchase Sites

Purchase sites are able to close sales online and only online. They are not affiliated with any physical store. Examples of purchase sites include Amazon.com, Buy.com, and Gettington.com.[14] Some purchase sites sell intangible goods, requiring no physical delivery. Examples include iTunes.com, MarketResearch.com, and E*TRADE.

Abandonment rates online are much higher than in physical stores. In some cases, over 50% of shopping carts are abandoned. In response to this challenge, marketers conduct a great deal of research and testing of the checkout process. Some sites are designed to jam as many shoppers as possible into the checkout process. When site responsibilities are divided, some sites may withhold information about the final terms, delivery, and account management in order to inflate the number of shoppers entering the checkout process. Under these circumstances, a high abandonment rate should be expected.

---

[14] Many of these companies call themselves ecommerce sties. However, that term has many meanings and often includes sites supporting sales in physical stores as well as online. The sales challenges are different, and a distinction needs to be made.

A portion of the problem may be some shoppers simply enter the checkout process without a deep sense of commitment. They may possess a curiosity to explore the checkout process when shopping on a site they never purchased from before. "If I do decide to buy it, what will be the process?"

The mystery behind shipping prices adds to the incidence of exploratory checkout. Shoppers may enter the checkout process just to obtain the total price or to confirm the "free shipping" offer is really free.

Aspects of account management may also require exploration. What is the return policy? Will I be able to take it back to one of their stores? Is there free shipping on returns? Will I receive an offer for discounts on future accessory purchases?

Debate and experimentation continues in this area. Should the site facilitate the shopper's ability to go in and out of the closing process with ease, or should every effort be made to maximize the close rates as a percentage of those entering the cart?

Sites choosing to do whatever it takes to maximize current profits need to monitor the impact of their choice over time. As consumers continue to take charge of the sales process and businesses build a culture of facilitating those consumers, it will become harder to maintain a "gotcha" close process. Looking at the lifecycle value of the customer tends to favor a continued recognition of the shopper's in-charge status.

Businesses run on profit, not the individual metrics contributing to a sale. Managers must be certain the site itself delivers an integrated sales process. In the example below, each system stands out as best in a particular measurement. If responsibility is divided, this results in a natural tendency toward conflict. Each team wants to maximize its own metric.

	System A	System B	System C
Percent of site visitors entering the checkout process	10%	13%	14%
Percent of checkouts completed	60%	50%	40%
Percent of site visitors completing the checkout process	6%	6.5%	5.6%
Percent increase in gross profit through up selling and cross selling in the checkout process	15%	0%	20%
Total gross profit	$6,900,000	$6,500,000	$6,720,000

System analytics are tricky and too often bent by internal politics. In this case, System A maximizes total profit during the period in question. System A may still not be the best system to choose. System B produced the most customers. If the product and system can deliver a great deal of loyalty and advocacy, System B might be the most profitable system on a life-cycle basis.

More will be said in Part 4 about the importance of functioning as a team and the fallacy of individual attribution. Systems measurement is essential for continual improvement, but systems measurement requires leadership. Results can bind a team together or rip it apart. Nothing is more destructive to teamwork than pay for individual performance. There is a reason baseball players are not rewarded based on the number of homeruns they hit. The objective of every hitter needs to be whatever it takes to best help the team win. As the sales process includes more touchpoints, more teamwork is essential.

The current focus of purchase sites appears to be more and more inventory. The focus must shift to more selling of whatever inventory is posted. Many sites limit product descriptions to 60-80 words. This may be ample for swimwear, but woefully insufficient for digital cameras. Cars.com now provides space for 32 product photos and 4000 characters of text for each vehicle.

Catalogs and Direct Mail

Print is usually reserved for information we do not expect to change during its useful life. Nothing is put into a Yellow Pages ad that will not be true through the expected shelf life of the publication. Any printed offers, coupons, or specials include expiration dates.

The popularity of print as a shopping medium emanates from its commitment, portability, and lasting presence. A great deal of thought goes into a product claim before it is put into writing. A written offer is irrefutable, provided it is clearly understood. A written offer can be taken to the store, shown to influencers, or handed to decision makers.

Arguably, information on a smart phone is equal to print in its commitment and even more portable. What cannot be denied is the superiority of print when it comes to presence. It can stay on the desk, countertop, or attached to the refrigerator as a constant reminder. Catalogs often serve as wish books. Products that are aspirational, yet ultimately attainable, are well suited for catalogs.

Direct mail is well suited for products with multiple stakeholders. It can be passed back and forth as an information source. In many cases, electronic content is even better suited for this purpose.

Printed catalogs and mail may decrease in volume and use, but the day of extinction remains distant. Consumers continue to bounce in and out of printed marketing material, sometimes to a close and sometimes to close through other touchpoints. Marketers must still consider printed material as they think through sales integration.

Chapter 14

Delivery Network

Delivery is the last touchpoint prior to product use and often makes a huge difference in the degree to which the consumer's quality of life is enhanced. Delivery is about far more than handing the product off to the shopper. Proper delivery enhances satisfaction, improves loyalty, and increases the likelihood of advocacy. This is the part of the sales process the business still controls, and every detail matters.

Much of the delivery is intangible. From the smile on the congratulating clerk or salesperson's face, to the explanation of the warranty and online assembly instruction, the importance of these intangible features of delivery cannot be overstated.

Integration with the internet can help establish expectations and avoid frustration. If a product requires assembly, instructions can be provided online. Pictures of what the package will look like, as well as the contents within the box may be important. Additionally, pictures of subassemblies can help the consumer envision how the packaged contents will come together to fulfill the promised result.

The same software being used to create employee training programs can be used to teach customers how to assemble and use products. While there is a cost to this kind of production, those costs are going down as the software becomes easier to use and quality photos and video are becoming cheaper and easier to produce. The advantages of greater customer satisfaction and more cross-sell opportunities can easily justify expense in many cases.[15]

Weber.com provides information about the outdoor cooking systems it sells through retailers. The site also sells parts and accessories directly. Providing interactive programs on how to assemble and operate products would increase shopper confidence about purchasing more complex products and provide additional opportunities for promoting parts and accessories.

Delivery of Intangible Products

The importance of delivery may be greatest when the product is intangible. The confirmation email or paperwork may be all the shopper has for the purchase, deposit, investment, or loan

---

[15] For examples of interactive assembly instructions, visit RevenueGuru.com

obligation. Scam artists love intangibles. Often, the understanding in the consumer or borrower's mind is very different from what the legal paperwork actually promises. Even when the understanding is clear, the consumer often purchases no more than a promise. Reassuring the consumer at the point of delivery is essential to customer satisfaction and the resulting loyalty and advocacy. A decision resulting in anxiety is a decision less likely to be repeated, even if the promise is delivered in full.

Mortgage companies don't need Federal regulators to tell them they must do more to assure borrowers their understanding of the terms are in fact what they think they are. The industry soils itself repeatedly. Better delivery can be used as a competitive advantage. Competition has the potential to instill higher standards than regulation ever can. For many people, regulation is for circumventing, and competition is for living up to or surpassing it.

Home Delivery

The quality of home delivery varies widely. The reactions inspired by home delivery can vary from "Is that it?" to "Wow, that's it!"

A pizza box carried in a stay-warm insulation container all the way to the doorstep will be perceived as not only warmer but of higher quality. When the delivery person waits until the last moment to expose the box, and does so with gestures indicating his or her pride in the product, the initial response is more likely to be favorable, and the monetary transaction more acceptable.

The body language, hand gestures, and facial expressions of the delivery person are important. Behavior indicating that physical movement of the pizza is all the delivery person feels responsible for diminishes the value of the pie relative to what it could be with proper delivery.

Appliances are too often delivered with "Sign here, it's at the bottom of the driveway." The "Where do you want it?" approach is not much better. It costs no more to deliver the product with an attitude that says, "Congratulations, we're proud to be the ones to present this to you!" If this sounds like a Pollyannaish thought, my response is, "When was the last time you tried?" Too few companies provide sales training to their delivery teams or insist the company the delivery is contracted out to should train its people. How many even tell their delivery people that they are part of the sales process?

Over 30 years ago, I sold bottled water door to door for Silver Springs. I traveled with a route owner and canvassed the neighborhood for new sales while he delivered to existing customers. The neighborhoods I worked were low income, and most of the people living there did not look like the driver or me. At the end of the day, we delivered to the homes I sold to that day. We knew our delivery had to be first rate. Done poorly, the deal could unwind. Done wonderfully and everyone in the apartment complex knew the Jones' were living large with bottled water. Neighbor children would beg their mothers, many just getting home from work, to buy from us right then and there. Get out on the front lines and see how your product is being delivered. The difference between what *is* and what *can be* may make all the difference in the world to your bottom line.

Of course, initial presentation is only a portion of a great home delivery. The product must arrive as expected, when expected. Consumers often assemble IKEA furniture in crowded apartments. IKEA.com provides information about the package measurement and weight, allowing the shopper to know what plans to make.

In-Store Delivery

The graphic below demonstrates the shift in tension occurring at the point of purchase. The way the store delivers the product makes all the difference in the world in how the consumer feels about their purchase, their likelihood to return for additional accessories, and their likelihood to recommend the store and/or product to friends and family members.

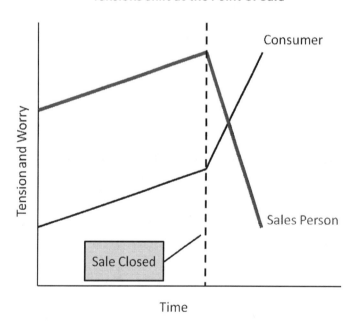

106

Within service industries, the importance of the initial point of delivery has long been understood. While I was research director for J.D. Power's Hospitality Group, it became clear through our consumer research that satisfaction with a hotel stay is largely influenced by the guest's experience at check-in and the initial cleanliness of the room. After the reservation is made to a new hotel, tensions may be high regarding fulfillment of that reservation. Will the room have the requested view? Will it have the requested amenities and configuration? Will it be as clean and elegant as advertised? As much as possible should be done to reassure consumers between reservation and arrival. Of course, upon arrival the delivery of service must come through as promised.

In many industries, the same recognition of delivery importance, with respect to product delivery, has yet to occur. The courtesy of helping shoppers get the product to and into their vehicle is long gone at many stores. The only person standing between the cash register and the door is a security guard trying to make sure you do not steal anything. Nearby are those customers who came back with a return or exchange being treated like they are a problem to the store. This is a poor last impression to send with the customer out the door.

One of the advantages of in-store delivery of products purchased online is the opportunity to sell additional products. If a retailer knows the shopper is going to pick a product up at the store, it makes sense to send an email letting the shopper know what accessory products or complementary goods are available at the store and where they can be found. A similar notification could be printed out and handed to the shopper at the time of pickup.

Delivery is suboptimal at most auto dealerships. Those selling the vehicles are typically paid a percentage of the gross profits from the deals they close. Once the customer agrees to buy the vehicle, thoughts are often focused on the next opportunity. From the short-term perspective of many sales people, no good can come from spending more time with the customer. Referrals take time to develop, and loyalty can take years to pay off. Many sales people working on commission see the next customer walking into the showroom as a bird in the hand, relative to whatever referrals may result from the delivery-process bush.

An effort is being made to utilize technology to fill this gap. In June of 2010, Ford Motor Company announced a new delivery program for their Fiesta product. It involves a combination MP3 player and USB that "unwraps" the vehicle for the consumer and attempts to engage them with Ford and the community of Fiesta owners at the point of delivery. The process is not entirely automated. It involves taking a picture of the buyer with their new vehicle.

Auto Dealer Carl Sewell literally wrote the book on customer service, *Customers for Life*. The book is a classic, but my experience visiting hundreds of stores and talking to many hundreds of dealers is the kind of delivery executed by the Sewell organization and articulated in Mr. Sewell's book is rarely imitated.

Curbside Pickup

Curbside pickup is a customer convenience with several faces. Many of the items not carried in stores carry that distinction because they are so very large. Anything too large to stock is probably too large to carry from the pickup counter in the back of the store to the parking lot without challenges. Curbside pickup is fantastic for large items.

On the other end of the spectrum, why should a shopper have to go into the store to hunt for the products he buys regularly? Going in and out of the store can be a problem in a number of circumstances. Leaving a hot yoga class, it may be a great deal more comfortable to order a few products through an iPhone application or a mobile website and pick them up at the curb.

The experiments Sears Holdings Corporation is conducting as part of its ShopYourWay program will be watched closely. Their Web to Store service offers in-store, curbside and third-party pickup options according to a press release issued March 13, 2010. Sears' total sales continue to decline, but online sales continued to increase even through the recession.

Change in shopping habits can take years before they are prevalent. DVD was introduced in 1997. Netflix began offering DVD rentals and sales in 1998, it took five years to reach 1,000,000 subscribers and enjoy its first quarterly profit. Today, the thought of going into a store to rent movies, the model Netflix and others destroyed, seems almost ridiculous; however, it was a habit not broken overnight. Similarly, the adoption rate for curbside pickup is difficult to predict.

Delivery Center

The UPS Store and Mail Boxes Etc. are examples of delivery centers. The primary purpose is to pick things up or send them out. Many online shoppers live in circumstances making home delivery unsafe or unsecure.

The future may bring many more delivery centers offering 24/7 service and handling an increasing share of the nation's commerce. If so, more thought will need to go into how retailers shipping to these sites can make the most of the experience and integrate it into the overall sales effort.

Delivery of Rental Products

The delivery of rental products is truly a tale of multiple service levels. I have rented many cars, tools, trucks, and trailers, as well as just about every type of power sports equipment known to man. I hang out near rental counters in airports and in marinas to listen in on delivery transactions. I am fascinated by just how bad delivery can be. Going from a rental car company at an airport, to a luxury hotel, and then to a company renting snowmobiles can be the ultimate rollercoaster in delivery service.

Member customers of national car rental companies generally have a pretty easy time taking delivery of a reserved vehicle. For non-members, or members caught in a snag, the process can be extremely frustrating. The industry is fraught with process problems and often staffed with people who simply execute policy. Solving problems is the last thing on their mind.

Having a reservation does not necessarily mean a vehicle is reserved for you. It is pretty hard for employees to execute a great vehicle delivery when they are out of vehicles. When a company's processes and policies treat customers poorly it does not take long for employees to catch on that corporate policy is king and any customer who cannot live with it is out of luck.

To their credit, some rental companies maintain a record of damaged areas on the vehicle. This is generally not the case for boat rentals. Before the customer leaves the dock, their first experience with the vessel is to try like the devil to find all the scratches and dings. If the customer spots it, they are in good shape. If they do not, they have no way of proving the damage did not occur on their watch. All the time the customer is going over the vessel finding problems, they know good and well any damage they find has already been paid for by another customer. Yet the lack of a database linked to the sales process means every customer must start their marine experience with this hide and seek game. There may be no way of getting around the customer walk through, but customers have a right to expect any damage worth reporting be repaired prior to their rental experience.

Most people tend to treat things the way the owners appear to treat them. This is well articulated in Malcolm Gladwell's popular book, *Tipping Point*. It stands to reason, making immediate expert repairs to damaged equipment is a good way of minimizing future damage. Delivery too often includes a story about the stupidity of the previous user who caused the damage, but rarely a demonstration of pride in how the product has been maintained and performs.

Economically, renting often makes far more sense than ownership. The performance level available in rental fleets continues to improve as well. One of the things holding this category back is the extraordinary differences in delivery. Some stores treat their customers like valued guests. Unfortunately, other companies treat their customers like idiots and hoodlums who are sure to do something stupid and damage the equipment. Are your delivery agents a part of an integrated sales process or are they equipment managers? If they have not been trained to deliver the product in a way that fosters loyalty and advocacy, then the answer is the latter.

International franchise organizations, like EagleRider, have an opportunity to establish a reputation for professional delivery that separates the brand from the many independent shops. Even if an independent shop provides a great delivery, the expectation in the minds of potential new customers may be tainted by previous encounters with other independent operators.

The internet allows rental companies an opportunity to demonstrate the delivery process online. Using the branching capabilities of interactive programs, it is possible to demonstrate the kind of delivery the shopper can expect based on their choices. The choice of insurance can be fully understood and made online. The difference in choices can be huge. One company renting ATVs requires a $5,000 deposit if their insurance is not purchased and a $1,000 deposit if purchased. Companies generally include helmets in the rental price. If a premium helmet is an available upgrade, facilitating that decision in the online demonstration and reservation processes can save time and heartache in the delivery process.

Chapter 15

Account Management

You cannot stop shoppers from bouncing across a multitude of websites, stores, and catalogs. You cannot limit their choices or the amount of information they see. Once they decide to purchase from your company, however, you can make it as easy as possible for them to get all the information they will need in order to get the most out of the product they purchased and the next one to come. The customer's next shopping process is no more in your hands than the first one, but great account management can deliver a level of preference over competitors.

Objectives of account management can include one or more of the following:

1. Continued payment
2. Sales of accessories (e.g. a portable microphone to a high-end video camera)
3. Sales of complementary products (e.g. a lighting system to make better videos with the camera)
4. Sales of products for people with similar needs or a similar lifestyle (e.g. variety of travel cases for serious video photographers)
5. Smooth off-lease transition (e.g. buy, trade-up, or return of a leased vehicle prior to lease termination date)
6. Customer satisfaction leading to another purchase by the customer
7. Customer satisfaction leading to a referral by the customer
8. Problem resolution to prevent negative ratings or comments from the customer

Each of these listed above lead to greater profits. The purpose of customer satisfaction is more loyalty and advocacy; therefore, account management systems must do more than satisfy customers. They must facilitate repeat purchases and referrals.

The newest and most interesting item may be the last. Loyalty and advocacy tend to come from ratings of 9 or 10 on a 10-point scale, or an 11-point scale using 0-10. Negative consumer ratings, however, can have a significant impact on future sales. Online ratings and reviews amplify the impact of negative testimony. More research needs to be done to determine the correlation between satisfaction ratings and the propensity to post a rating online. The act of posting a rating is very different from talking about it. Some shoppers feel an almost religious obligation to post reviews. Some consumers never consider posting a review until they experience something miraculously wonderful or extremely disappointing.

Online ratings are changing both the propensity to inject negative ratings, their amplification, and their endurance. Business managers must be cognizant of what causes negative ratings. Along with improving the processes that lead to negative ratings, managers must develop account management systems that help minimize the quantity and impact of negative ratings.

The validity of Net Promoter Scores (NPS) is now in question.[16] On a scale of 0-10, is a person answering a survey with a satisfaction rating of 6 equally likely to post a negative rating online as a person answering the survey with a score of 0? Is the positive impact on future growth from a Promoter equal to the negative impact of a Detractor? How is this changing over time? NPS has always been controversial. It may very well be time to go back to using all the data and stop pretending the impact of a distribution can be consistently predicted with a single metric. The internet's impact on promotion and detraction will continue to develop, but likely not at the same pace. Account management functions must impact both ends of the satisfaction scale and monitor them both as well.

Some online accounts simply lay dormant until the shopper comes back to purchase something. This is fine for huge online retailers, like Amazon. Websites offering a limited line of infrequently shopped goods need to work a bit harder. Offering information that will enhance the consumer's quality of life helps get them back to the sites more frequently. Sears provides ManageMyLife.com, offering information and expert answers to questions. It facilitates community interaction. Shoppers can download product manuals from the site. It also provides project designs and advice.

Periodically reaching out to customers may be an old-fashioned method of account management; however, it can be very effective when combined with a robust CRM system. This is particularly important for products requiring maintenance. A gentle reminder via phone or email to let the customer know it is time for an oil change, tire rotation, or any other scheduled maintenance can help retain business. This should not be a cold call. If the customer was introduced to a service manager at the time of delivery, this is a helpful call from someone who cares.

One of the functions of physical stores is to provide a place where customers can return when problems arise. Unfortunately, as more and more business moves online for banks and other institutions, the trend seems to be to make physical locations less and less empowered. This is exactly the opposite of what should be happening.

---

[16] Net Promoter is a registered trademark of Fred Reichheld, Bain & Company, and Satmetix. The metric was introduced in Fred Reichheld's 2003 Harvard Business Review article, "The One Number You Need to Grow." The results from a scale of 0-10 are aggregated into three groups, Promoters (9-10), Passives (7-8), Detractors (0-6). The percentage of Detractors is subtracted from the percentage of Promoters for a final score.

As physical locations are accessed less for day-to-day transactions, they become more essential for exceptional needs. Many consumers happily manage large accounts online, but that does not mean the face-to-face interaction is not as important as ever when problems do arise. Scaling down physical locations as volume there decreases may be a mistake. The function of these locations needs to be redefined. Indeed, a higher percentage of the transactions handled in bank locations are of a sensitive nature, now that many routine transactions moved online.

Chapter 16

Horizontal Sales Integration

In many cases, consumers require a bundle of products and services. A vehicle sale may include accessories, a warranty, and a variety of financial products including lending and insurance. Some products require services for installation or modification, as well as maintenance. Whether or not the retailer offers all of these products and services, if they are important to the customer, they must be addressed in the sales process.

On the surface, integrating the sale of products, services, warranties and finance products may appear simple. The reality is these sales are often isolated. By obtaining a commitment on the core product first, the shopper becomes easier prey for high margin warranties and accessories. After the commitment is made for jewelry or appliances, a warranty is offered at an additional price. After the mobile phone is selected, accessories are introduced. After the customer commits to buying a vehicle, they are sent to the F&I (Finance and Insurance) desk.

When the entire sales process took place in the store, this linear approach made sense for merchants. Once the commitment to buy the core product was secure, complementary products could more easily be piled on with larger margins. It was not unusual to sell theft protection devices through auto dealerships at markups of 300%.

Today, shoppers can obtain market information about finance rates, warranty costs, security systems, and accessories online at any time in the shopping process. In the store, shoppers might fear they appear rude if they inquired about the costs of extended warranties and finance rates associated with each vehicle they consider. Online, shoppers are free to spend countless hours constructing bundles as they wish.

Shoppers can compare costs from multiple vendors for each element of their chosen bundle. Even if shoppers have a desire to purchase the entire bundle from one source, transparency of information allows them to compare rates and negotiate with full knowledge of their alternatives. If pricing is not disclosed online for all elements of the bundle, the merchant risks losing the shopper to a competitor who does meet those information needs.

Increasingly, the lack of transparency from one retailer will be used against it by another. Auto dealers are infamous for adding processing or document fees not disclosed until it is time to sign the agreement. Battison Auto Group makes a point of reminding shoppers early in the shopping process of their no fees policy. Not only does this position Battison as more forthcoming, it reminds the shopper they do not know what the total cost of the bundle will be from other retailers, even if the vehicle prices are clearly posted.

Brands like Scion offer lots of options and accessories. Upselling accessories can bring as much to a retailer's bottom line as the purchase of the base product itself. This is the case in high-end cameras and other durable goods. Early on in the shopping process, consumers need access to information about how these accessories will be made available to them.

The manufacturer dictates what accessories will nullify the warranty. Longer warranties in the automobile industry gave manufacturers renewed power with respect to accessories. This builds in a strong preference for accessories offered by the manufacturer, even if they are premium priced. The warranty nullification issue sends two powerful signals in the same direction. It clearly says the loss of warranty benefits might be prohibitive, and it says aftermarket products may damage the product. If the manufacturer goes too far, however, shoppers may get the impression they are simply being penned in by the manufacturer.

Product and Service from Different Companies

What happens when a shopper wants a very special stained glass window and wants it installed? The shopper wants a price and installation date for the entire package. They may want to buy the window from ChurchInteriors.com and have someone from the local community provide the installation.

Wouldn't it be great if the shopper could press a button and solicit bids from installation providers for that exact product? This could be a system that includes all the required information for bidding the installation. The product information, like dimensions and weight, come from the product company database. Information about the installation location (address, access, work height, etc.) is input into a form by the shopper. The package is then sent to various service providers for installation bids.

It is hard to find examples of great horizontal integration, yet it is so easy to find places where it can be improved. A company selling backyard play sets might provide information about options for ground covering. If pea gravel is a good option, how deep should it be? If it is sold by the ton, how many cubic yards are in a ton. Better yet would be a tool or chart for calculating the amount needed when the depth and number of square feet are determined.

SwingSetSource.com sells recycled rubber mulch for $979.98 (regularly $1,299.99) per ton. The site clearly states one ton will cover 300 square feet to 3 inches deep. WillyGoat.com sells the playground boarder kits to put the filler in, but not the filler itself. Nor do they say where to buy it, how to buy it, how much to buy, or what kind is recommended.

Cedarworks.com sells high-end sets that are splinter-free, chemical-free, and maintenance-free. Everything about the sites says its products are for people who want the best for their children. On the issue of ground surface, the site points out that the Consumer Product Safety Commission recommends all sets be on loose-fill material, like wood chips or pea stone. Unfortunately, there is no more information than that. This site that is otherwise so caring of people might as well say, "go figure it out, we don't profit from that part of the business."

If you rely on the seller of the complementary good to sell to your customer properly, then you might still get your sale. If you provide all the tools and information your customer will need, you will close more sales and receive far more referrals.

Horizontal Integration as a Competitive Advantage

Lack of horizontal sales integration has been a huge problem in some industries for a long time. Most shoppers feel they would receive a better price on a late-model used vehicle from a private party than from a dealer. Only 11% of these shoppers actually buy from a private party, however. The primary advantage dealerships have is the ability to integrate the sales process horizontally.

The purchase of a home is extremely important and the horizontal integration is frustratingly poor. When problems arise, the Realtor blames the lender. The title insurance company blames both. Everyone blames the inspectors and appraisers, who feel accountable to no one. Describing the process ahead of time in common language does not remove the potential for problems, but it can lessen the intensity of the frustration. Realtors who prepare their customer, particularly first-time buyers, will be more apt to earn their advocacy.

Part 4

Moving Forward

Chapter 17

Pricing and Demonstrating Value

Pre-built products must be clearly and consistently priced across all touchpoints. The notion of holding out a price to entice the shopper to take the next step in the purchase funnel is consistent with the myths of a linear shopping process and seller control. Sales integration requires consistent and transparent pricing.

Shoppers want to know price for two reasons:

1. Affordability
2. Determining comparative value

If your product is more than the shopper can afford, you do not have a reasonable chance of obtaining a sale. If showing the price alienates these shoppers it is not loss. In a world of increasing transparency, no marketer can opt out of value comparisons. Provide the price and the value demonstration.

Some products come with a multitude of options. If there are a lot of variables contributing to price, then the marketer must provide an online tool for determining price at as many touchpoints as possible. Industries like autos and motorcycles have partially stepped up to this challenge with configurators on manufacturer, dealer, and independent websites. Unfortunately, the result is often only the MSRP and not the offer price. Services like Ai-Dealer are beginning to change that with a configurator leading to an offer price. Ai-Dealer's shopping cart provides the shopper an opportunity to construct the entire bundle, including F&I, with transparent pricing and purchase the vehicle online or at the store.

Residential eldercare provides virtually no online pricing other than price ranges so wide as to be nearly useless in many cases. Making value comparisons for assisted living arrangements is frustratingly difficult and time consuming. The amount of business lost to hospice care and home monitoring systems due to the extreme frustration with the shopping process is unknown, but it is safe to say millions of dollars per month are being diverted from the residential side of this industry because of poor sales integration, particularly the unwillingness to generate prices online.

Some custom products and services are more complicated to generate a pricing tool for than the effort is worth. One approach is to provide a useful, estimated price range. Another is to provide a bottom price with an example of the kinds of customizations available and some guidance as to how they impact price. Yet another approach for customized products and services is to provide details of completed products – sold or available – with prices.

CustomMade.com provides directories by craft and location. Within each artisan's gallery of photo samples, an estimated cost to produce something similar is provided in the form of a price range. There is also a matchmaking section taking the shopper through a series of questions in order to put them in touch with the right artisans.

Burdick Custom Homes provides photos and floor plans of completed projects available for sale. They also provide floor plans and artist renderings for those not yet built. Most of the available inventory and plans include pricing, providing some degree of guidance for shoppers wanting something truly custom.

Pollaro Custom Furniture makes museum quality furniture and offers no prices on Pollaro.com. This may be appropriate for extremely high-end products. Unless your custom products are truly priceless, it is best to put a price on them.

Many high-end bakeries do not provide any online pricing guidance for their wedding cakes. This may work for a long established firm living off reputation and referral business. In these cases, the website may be little more than a brag book. Lack of pricing may confirm the status associated with purchasing edible artwork from a particular baker/artisan. It also sends the message that status comes at a premium price. Ultimately, snobbery has a price. Creative Cakes provides cost-per-serving guidance for cake, icing, coverings, and fillings on CreativeCakes.com. The Silver Spring MD shop is less status oriented, and the website clearly facilitates the sales process.

Price Discrimination

When consumers lacked transparency into the market, negotiating the price made perfect sense for many merchants of infrequently purchased products. Price discrimination – charging different customers different prices for the same product through the same distribution channel – maximizes gross profits. Additionally, the effort involved in negotiating raised the exit barriers for shoppers – do the deal or start over somewhere else.

With transparency into market prices, negotiating does not make as much sense as it once did. Posting a higher starting price, rather than an aggressive offer price, results in fewer shoppers contacting the store. Shoppers carry the market prices around with them in their internet-enabled phones, so the switching cost is lower than it was. As more and more merchants move to an aggressive one-price approach, the consumer has greater knowledge of their options. For competing stores leaving themselves a margin for negotiations, the result is less traffic to the store and tougher negotiations with those who do come.

There is a tipping point in any community. When enough stores begin posting their best price online, every store needs to do it. Within the auto industry, the St. Paul-Minneapolis market is quickly reaching that point. Those dealers who do it first and focus their branding advertising around this positioning have a sustained competitive advantage. From a purely economic perspective, it is clear that price discrimination is eventually on its way out in any industry where inventory prices are commonly posted online.

This movement toward putting the best price up front would be moving even faster if dealers knew the consequences. Most auto dealers are not economists, and they have little transparency into the impact of switching pricing strategies. Worse yet, many dealers report taking an initial loss through the transition period. More than one dealer has switched to a one-price operation, switched back, and then discovered they needed to switch again.

Most of the large dealer groups are shifting toward a single price, or one with very little room for negotiations, as documented repeatedly in the leading trade publication, *Automotive News*. Dealer groups operating with multiple brands across multiple communities possess the advantage of being able to compare bottom line results of various strategies executed across their network of stores. Single-store operations lack this insight, but most are very bright and will follow as a critical mass develops in their community and the profitability of the current system quickly dwindles.

What is true in autos is true in any industry. The ability to post prices online ultimately destroys the price discrimination model. The first wave is the need to post priced inventory online in order to sustain store traffic. The second wave brings the need to price aggressively – best price upfront. As consumers become accustomed to shopping this way for autos and other durable goods, they will demand the same in other industries. Lagging industries may find the transition moves much faster for them when it does come.

The shift away from price discrimination will change the makeup of the sales force. With price discrimination, the ability to negotiate effectively was an important skill. Development of this skill took time, posing a problem for sales teams facing annual turnover in excess of 100%. CarMax, an early adopter of fixed pricing, does not have to search and compete for salespeople with the ability to negotiate effectively.

As margins compress and less emphasis is placed on negations, compensation changes as well. Automobile sales professionals were commonly paid 20-25% of the gross profit with occasional spiffs on hard-to-move inventory. There was no base salary. Every dime in the salesperson's pocket came from commission, and the incentive to hold gross was high. An additional discount of $500 is only 1% off on a $50,000 vehicle; however; it may be a reduction of 10-30% of the remaining gross profit.

It is becoming increasingly common for sales professionals to be paid a base salary plus commission. Frequently, the commission is based on unit volume, rather than gross profit. Clearly, once the gross profit is fixed the link to compensation based on gross profit is necessarily broken.

The likely progression is greater emphasis on the sale of high-margin accessories in addition to unit sales. This requires greater listening skills, broader product knowledge, and more demonstration skills. These skills benefit the shopper in a profit generating way. Negotiations, although not adversarial when properly done, often produce little benefit to the customer.

Dale Pollak, author of *Velocity* and *Velocity 2.0*, makes the point that documentation is the new negotiations. His work is focused on used cars, but the point is valid for any substantial purchase. The merchant must demonstrate the value of the product. Its price is known, and competing prices are known. Providing credible evidence to support your claim that the product is a superior value is essential. This information should be available online and the sales force must learn how to utilize documents to demonstrate value as the need for negotiating skills drifts away.

Demonstrating Product Value

If you offer something free, you need to demonstrate the full value. Southwest Airlines advertises the heck out of the fact they do not charge for luggage. They have to. Otherwise, shoppers will compare rates that are apples and oranges. If Southwest can get shoppers upset enough about baggage charges, shoppers may not even consider airlines that charge. The fact that Southwest reservations are only obtained through Southwest, lines up with this strategy.

Zappos.com must make a big deal about its policy of free shipping and free returns. It must do so in order to enhance perceived value and establish preference for the site.

When the price of core products, like flights or shoes, are posted online, there is a temptation to slim down the core price and make up the difference with additional changes. This follows the tactics used for products sold on television based on price. Everything is about the amazing value, then the outrageous shipping and handling charge is quietly mentioned at the end. Such tactics open the door for competitors to focus communication on the fact they don't charge extra for the thing that made the customer feel cheated (e.g. baggage fees or excess shipping changes).

If a company is going to deviate from the industry standard, it should go all the way. If you are the only site in your industry charging shipping, are your product prices always guaranteed to be the lowest? If everyone charges for shipping or baggage, do not make your charges less, eliminate them entirely. Customers are sensitive about some dollars more than others. Charging an extra dollar for the steak would be a great deal more tolerable than charging a dollar for the tap water. Free shipping for a product may not mean much if others are shipping at cost. If shoppers are feeling gouged by shipping cost, then there is an opportunity to capitalize with free shipping. Find out which dollars customers are most sensitive about in your industry and you may be able to gain a competitive advantage by going the other way.

Information and checkout processes are similar. If shoppers are upset by having to submit a form in order to get a quote, figure out how to meet their information needs easier. If a long checkout process loaded with cross-sell options frustrates shoppers, then move to a shopping cart with single-page checkout.

Many online shopping sites offer "specials," products that allow the shopper to look at a computer generated consideration set of closely related products from the same retailer. This helps the shopper become more confident the retailer has relevant inventory to meet their needs if they do change their mind about what to buy. Each listing for a new product should show which additional colors, options, and features are available from the same retailer and what price range the retailer offers within this model line. If the site you are posting inventory on does not provide this tool, then include this information in the text description if possible.

Accessories can account for a higher share of the gross profit than the core unit can. Accessories, insurance, and financing may account for more than 100% of the profit in a very competitive market. Honda's Big Red multipurpose utility vehicle has a base price of $11,699. Powersports.Honda.com offers 37 accessories for this vehicle worth $7,202. The website's configurator offers each accessory with a photo, price, and text description. The descriptions do not sell to the extent they should, but the demonstrations are as good as most. Dealers carrying the product should do at least as much to sell the accessories and capitalize on the margins and potential instillation work they provide.

Providing accessories availability, pricing, and great product descriptions is essential for facilitating the shopper's sales process and maximizing profits. Automobile manufacturers seem mystified by the fact that most accessories are not purchased through their dealers. Yet, like Honda's power sports site, the configurator is the only place specific vehicle accessories can be found. General use accessories, like lubricants and apparel are not included in the configurator.

Of course, little of this matters if the vehicle salesperson is not trained or compensated for the sale of accessories. Accessories are often purchased before the first oil change. Losing accessory sales to retailers with no tie to the manufacturer may move the relationship and threaten future service sales, as well.

Demonstrating Retailer Value

With the ability to see what the market offers and how those products are priced, consumers often find a consideration set of products they value equally at their given prices. If value is defined as benefits divided by price, we can see that some products have fewer features or lower perceived quality, but at a lower price than superior products. When the shopper has a consideration set of products they are indifferent to, they have reached value parity. As consumers gain greater and greater transparency into the market, value parity occurs more frequently.

It is important retailers demonstrate why they are the right company from which to buy. If the shopper has a consideration set of three products he feels represent equal value, then the retailer receiving the first call will likely be the one that best demonstrates its value.

If two dresses have the same overall value to the shopper regardless of where they are purchased, then the dress at Nordstrom's is probably going to be chosen over the one at Sears. How much more of a differentiator is the retailer for a durable goods purchase that may require post-purchase interaction for training, parts, service, warranty work, and more? Demonstrating your store is the best to buy from may require demonstrations in all of these areas.

Just when the shopper is being bombarded with nearly all of the product variation he can absorb, the internet makes it possible to compare products better than ever. An ATV shopper may be indifferent to the Kawasaki 2009 Brute Force® 750 NRA Outdoors™ at $8,949 and the Suzuki King Quad 750A Xi Rockstar Edition at $7,999. The products have a great deal of differentiation, but that can be understood and compared by the shopper better and more easily than ever. The prices are different, but the values represented may be the same for that unique shopper. This is a clear case of value parity. The dealer and the manufacturer that get the sale will be the one with the best retail value added. In this way, the strength of a manufacturer's retail network – both online and offline – will have an increasing impact on manufacturer sales as shoppers make better use of their market transparency and product value differences collapse.

The concept of demonstrating the value added by the retailer extends to online purchases as well. Sites like Shopping.com may show a multitude of retailers offering the same product. The one with the lowest price does not always receive the order. Some sites have higher ratings from past customers. Some offer free shipping. Some provide a hassle-free return policy.

The increasing frequency of value parity will continue to put more emphasis on retailers' reputations and their ability to demonstrate their value-add. In a transparent market, the value added by the retailer must be documented rather than just claimed.

Carfolks.com allows shoppers to submit and read reviews for any dealer in the nation. Participating dealers have the ability to demonstrate their sales teams with photographs and descriptions of each salesperson. Best of all, shoppers can read and submit ratings and reviews for individual sales professionals. Often the variation in customer satisfaction has more to do with finding the right salesperson within the store than finding the right store.

Typically, when a shopper drives up without an appointment or a requested salesperson, they are served by whichever salesperson has the next turn. This is known in the industry as the "ups" system. Consumers without an appointment are often referred to as ups by the sales team. Many shoppers are wise to this and would prefer to choose their automotive salesperson, much like they choose a realtor. By providing information about each salesperson online, the shopper is likely to prefer at least one of those individuals to rolling the dice at another store.

According to officials at Carfolks.com, the concept of providing salesperson level details and ratings came from a presentation I made at a dealer conference in 2005. It went something like this:

> I can go to Walmart and buy a $2.00 loaf of bread from any cashier I want to. If I'm by myself, I choose the cute one no matter how long the line is. If I'm with Mrs. Galbraith, I choose a cashier older and less pretty just to keep things right at home. The point is I get to pick who I buy my bread from.

> I come into the dealership to buy a $40,000 automobile and I'm an up for whatever pimply faced geek whose turn it is. The shopper spends hours shopping online in control of the sales process, then this. They pick their realtor, they pick their Walmart cashier, and they want to pick who they are going to spend several hours of their life and more than half a year's salary with. Give them that opportunity and do it online.

The added benefit to the dealership is their sales team knows each one of them will receive reviews. They know their appearance in the photo had better be well groomed, and they will need to match that expectation when shoppers meet them at the store.

The auto industry is not alone in its need for personnel detail. Most durable goods fall into this category. Gift shopping can also be very uncomfortable. Like many men, I would not be caught dead in a Victoria's Secret store, unless I had an appointment with someone with a reputation for professionalism and minimizing embarrassment. Waiters and waitresses, hairstylists, and other service providers might take their service to a higher level and earn more business with this kind of transparency into their service performance.

Every store and every site with a "Buy Now" button needs to demonstrate why they are the right merchant to close the deal. At RevenueGuru.com, we are just beginning to experiment with interactive programs designed to allow the shopper to explore the benefits of the retailer. The use of sight, sound, and motion should provide an engagement level that transfers information and stimulates emotions quickly. The interactive nature of the program puts the shopper more in control than standard video demonstrations. Regardless of how it is done, the need to demonstrate the added value of the retailer will increase as greater transparency leads to more incidence of value parity.

The foundation for these demonstrations must be the store's performance rather than its claims. Whatever means one chooses to demonstrate the store is the right one to buy from, it will need to live up to the claims made. Ratings are something a merchant can easily monitor, but negative comments in the world of social media can be destructive.

Chapter 18

The Year 2022

Sally goes online to shop for her daughter's Quinceañera. Having married into the Hispanic culture, she is eager to shop as intelligently as possible before exposing her choices to the scrutiny of her mother-in-law and her husband's cousins. Her new home is spacious with a large back yard. She is eager to show it off, but wants improvements before the event. Today she needs a cake, centerpieces, and a landscape architect.

The Cake

She begins at a search engine, which takes her to an information site about Quinceañeras. She spends more than an hour going back and forth from articles and videos back to the site. Then she goes back to the search engine for another information site, then more articles and occasionally linking to vendors through hyperlinks in the text adjacent to videos, and in adjacent ads.

With still no idea what she would like the cake to look like; she knows what message she wants to send. An independent site for bakeries provides detailed information about each shop. The shop's gallery of cake photos includes text or audio narration that can be opted into. The designer gives some background about what the buyer was looking for and the process the designer took to listen and meet those needs. A program using data from the CRM populated the information. The designer simply reviews the description and makes modifications. After the modifications are made, she can accept the audio track that is automatically generated or record her own using the text as script.

Sally narrows her selection of designers down to three who truly understand the Quinceañera celebration and seem like the kind of people who would listen to her and understand her needs. One of the designers got her start when helping her stepmother plan the ceremony for her younger half sister. As Sally watches the brief video of the designer's philosophy and approach, she feels a sense of bonding and understanding before even meeting the woman.

The cake designer knows her past achievements pale in comparison to her ability to help the shopper accomplish what she wants and needs. She understands much of the sales process will happen before she ever meets the shopper, as the shopper interacts with the content she created. The designer knew as she created the content her actions were not interruption advertising. The people coming to her site want to buy; they want to control the sales process; and they want the bakery to invest time into their sales process in the form of relevant content that is easy to find and free to explore.

It is Saturday and the younger children are both noisy and nosy. Sally chooses to make her initial contact with the baker through chat. The shop agent, Fran, asks Sally if she would mind giving her the code that has been persistently visible throughout the call. By providing the code in her chat session, Sally is able to send the click-stream history of this site visitation to Fran. Fran now has four screens open in separate monitors. She can seen the chat in one, the history of Sally's shopping in another, the screen Sally is looking at in a third, and the live site as Fran controls in a fourth.

Essentially, Fran's visual channel is able to see where Sally was, where she is, and where she wants Sally to go next, all while communicating with her in the chat. If needed, she can activate a program translating Sally's chats into real-time audio output and/or translating Fran's voice into real-time text output for Sally. The limitations of Sally's environment dictate the terms of the engagement, but Fran is able to control how she participates, taking full advantage of her environment to maximize listening and learning.

From her training, Fran knows a sales conversation is a learning process for both shopper and seller. The shopper makes the contact because they do not yet have sufficient information and confidence to make the decision. The seller needs to learn what the shopper needs in order to help them. By allowing both parties to take in the relevant information through both their audio and visual channels, learning is maximized for both parties to the extent permitted by the uncontrolled elements of the environment.

Of course, Sally was hoping to make contact with the designer, but she is not available at this time. Fran's sales training went far beyond product knowledge. She knows the culture of the shop, what the site says, and about the designer. With a few softly probing questions, Fran understands why Sally chose to call her shop first and is able to empathize with her.

The two women work together through a simple to use Computer Aided Design (CAD) program on which Fran is trained. She provides real-time access to what she is creating as Sally looks on and talks her through her thoughts and preferences. As they work through the design, both women can see the total cost of the cake change and the incremental impact on price from the latest change. The transparency Sally enjoyed in her autonomous sales process is now extended over to the sales process she has invited Fran into. Sally has given up nothing to interact with a salesperson, a note she will include to her friends as she enters a post about the experience later this evening.

Sally is torn between two cakes. She strongly feels it would be better to approach her husband's family with a short list of acceptable alternatives than a final choice. A date is scheduled for Fran to introduce Sally to the designer at the shop. Prior to the meeting, the designer will have access to the chat transcripts, related screen shots, and cake designs in the CRM system. She will confirm her ability to create each cake and the price of doing so prior to her call with Fran and Sally.

As Sally and the designer close the deal, they also arrange the optimal delivery. The cake will come in a clean, bright refrigerated van with all the markings of a specialty bakery. It will be advertising for the shop and Sally. The entire neighborhood will know just how special the day's event is going to be and which bakery was chosen as the best. The cake will be offloaded two hours prior to the event in an insulated stainless steel container with a cooling pack. The container maintains the freshness of the cake and the element of surprise. Sally understands and appreciates these benefits.

The surprise to Sally will be the attitude of the delivery. The cake will be handled like the newborn that it is. The precious and valuable nature of the cargo so delicately protected within the container will be more than evident from down the street in each direction.

The direction from Sally is an act the delivery professionals gladly respond to in the appropriate manner. They already know what to do, where to go, and who to talk to. The delivery is truly integrated into, and a vital part of, the sales process. It is part of what adds value to the product. The shop owner knows that the mannerism of her delivery people impact the perceived appearance and flavor of the cake. The senses of her customers are intertwined as they receive and process information. This experience will be embedded in the long-term memory of her customer. Sally is likely to remember the details of this day and this cake far better than most. She will certainly recall the things that stimulated positive emotions for a very long time to come.

Sally agrees to a follow-up phone call from the designer. She will be thrilled and will accept quarterly distribution of the bakery's newsletter. She will receive a photo of the cake as it was in the bakery alongside the proud designer. Sally will also receive the frame of her choice engraved with the name of the bakery. The designer will invite Sally to tag the shop in her social media and link to the picture there. These are just the beginning elements of an account management program that will be recorded in the CRM system and generate loyalty and advocacy for years to come.

Sally will be encouraged to provide a positive rating and comment on an independent website collecting and displaying ratings. The bakery monitors its reputation closely and responds to negative reviews with non-defensive language and sincere efforts to make things right. Primarily, the shop manages its reputation proactively by providing a great sales experience. Their definition of a great sales experience is one that easily facilitates the shopper's quest for the right cake in the right place at the right time delivered in the right way, with easy access to all of the right information so the shopper can confidently make the purchase.

Twelve years ago, in 2010, the use of these tools in a closed-loop system would have seemed prohibitively expensive for a local bakery. Now it is routine. The software providing a superior selling process consumes no resources. The product will be ideal, yet its enhanced value will have virtually no carbon footprint. Compared to an off-the-shelf cake, the only things added to the development of the cake were superior communications and design. Yet Fran and her company double the price of the cake, and the value of it tripled for Sally and her family. It is, as her daughter will remark on the day of the celebration, "the perfect cake."

The Centerpieces

Again Sally's search begins online, and again she bounces from site to site as she pleases. After searching and exploring for 45 minutes across 12 different websites, some several times, she thinks she found the perfect centerpiece. She can have an order shipped to her home or pick it up at the store. The challenge is uncertainty about what the in-laws will think. She could forward a complete description to each of her family advisers, but decides a physical sample is best for those she will see tomorrow.

From the manufacturer's product description, she is able to identify a nearby store that carries the product and has it in stock. Like so many things, the store price is identical to the shipped price. She just wants a single sample at this time, and the store is on the way to her youngest daughter's soccer game.

When she gets to the store, finding the product is a snap. Her internet-enabled mobile phone is equipped with an identifier for Radio-frequency identification (RFID) tags. The modern GPS guides her through the store to the product. Her phone also confirms the price of the product and allows her to self-pay as she walks out the door with product in hand.

After conferring with the band of family advisors, the centerpieces will be a go. The information provided online will help Sally convince her mother-in-law the symbol of purity displayed on the centerpiece is not some secret code among young people, but something actually looked favorably upon by their church. The cousins will like that it is modern and mother will appreciate that it contains traditional messaging.

Sally needs 20 of the centerpieces and will place her order. For both environmental and national security reasons, Sally does not like burning any more fuel than necessary. The retailer's website includes a calculator to measure which delivery method would consume the least fuel, Sally stopping by the store or the delivery person's stopping by the house. The difference may be only a few drops of fuel, but the calculation takes but a click to perform. The online calculator pulls all the necessary information from a personal database, but only after she allows temporary access to this data from the secure website. She chooses curbside pickup at the store.

Sally is very accustomed to curbside pickup. By pressing a pre-programmed button on her steering wheel, her phone sends a text message to the store notifying them of her expected arrival time. When she arrives, the product will be waiting at curbside and the attendant places it inside. There is no downtime for the transaction. The attendant's confirmation of delivery shows up on Sally's dashboard monitor. A second notice lets her know the electronic receipt has arrived in her personal accounting inbox.

Although the order will be packaged properly, the curbside attendant will also handle the box with care. The contents are both fragile and of a sentimental nature. The attendant knows from his training his service and the way he handles the customer's product adds value. He knows it is his job to enhance quality of life for all stakeholders and takes pride in his ability to deliver. Sally's order will be one of many that day, but he will treat her as if her order is the only thing that matters to him at that moment in time. His eye contact and movements will be deliberate at the time of delivery. He cares about his customer and is proud of his company's product.

If something should change, Sally can return the centerpieces either through the store or by shipping them. Although Sally's only human interaction will be with the curbside attendant, her shopping information is attached to her account. When shopping online, the retailer's website inquired about the event the centerpieces were intended for. Ordinarily, well wishes would be sent out electronically to Sally's daughter. Sally does not wish to opt in to this feature, however, controlling the flow of information to her daughter's inbox.

The interactions the shopper has with the various software systems have virtually no variable cost or resource expenditure. Such systems are now commonplace in the year 2022, and integration problems are largely a thing of the past. Shopper data is stored in a standard manner. Not only is Sally's sales process faster and easier than it was in 2010, the vendor costs are lower and profit margins improved.

The Landscape Architect

Sally's sense of responsibility toward the environment was on her mind as she thought about what could be done to beautify her spacious back yard before the celebration. It should be impressive, utilitarian, and responsible, but how would that translate into a finished product? How much time do such things take? What would be the cost? What was she not considering that she should be? Her head was abuzz.

Years ago, there was little to guide the shopping process for a landscape architect, other than the laborious exploration from site to site. In 2022, the world is a much better place to live, and shopping for professional services has never been easier.

Through a search engine, Sally found several sites providing guidance about how to shop for a landscape architect and a directory of them with detailed listings. She was quickly able to narrow her choices down to those who specialized in residential work and demonstrated a concern for the environment. Browsing through the listings across a single site was easy enough, but shopping tools made it possible to compare a list of services across the attributes most important to Sally.

Along the way, she stumbled across a picture full of children and some information about multisensory exploration. Although her children were growing beyond the age of playground exhibits, she intended to increase the amount of entertaining her immediate family did with others who have children. The coming celebration for her daughter would be such an occasion. Additionally, one of her husband's cousins had a special needs child Sally had grown very fond of. Yes, there should be room for something the smaller children will enjoy and learn from.

The architect Sally liked most, based on her online shopping, was Mike. He was local and seemed equipped to meet most of Sally's needs. Unfortunately, he did not appear to have experience in providing backyard toys designed to expand the development of multisensory exploration. Then she noticed Mike was linked to several other firms and organizations, one of which was a company that did specialize in play equipment and clearly understood special needs children. What a find! Might Mike be able to lead the project and tap into the additional specialties she needed?

As a one-person shop, Mike fully understands the benefits of horizontal sales integration. Often, his clients need more than his expertise can provide. By demonstrating the capabilities of partnering companies on his website, he is able to convince shoppers like Sally he has what it takes to do the job. He closes more business and receives the lead role on the project most of the time.

Mike also knows horizontal integration means an additional emphasis on listening. He will need to fully understand Sally's needs and his partner's capability. Making sure his partner's delivery is performed to Sally's expectations is a challenge. Mike provides his partners with interactive training programs so their people know what is expected of them when they work on one of his jobs and communicate with his customers.

When Mike takes the call on his mobile phone, it is automatically entered into his CRM along with some recorded notes he makes into his phone after the call. The recording is instantly available in its audio form or as a printable transcript. From the text format, various facts are lined up with fields in the CRM. Mike can accept them all at once or review each individually.

By the time Mike closes the deal, his CRM will have more information on Sally and her home than any competing landscape architect could hope for. He will simultaneously work toward a closed sale and a customer for life.

The CRM makes it easy to export information to vendors and subcontractors as needed. It also appends warranty and other information from the vendors to Sally's file. Should a problem arise, Mike will look like the most organized one-person shop imaginable.

During their meeting, Mike will show Sally what her yard can look like by manipulating the Computer Aided Design (CAD) program right before her eyes. The design tools now have multiple interfaces, one for use in the sales process and one for details and proprietary information.

To stimulate referral business, Mike will take pictures of Sally and her Husband in the completed yard. He will send her the gallery of photos and encourage her to post them on her social media sites along with a few candid words about the service she received. Mike knows a very low percentage of social media posts have anything to do with products, but this will be a custom job with Sally's signature all over it. He will take the time to facilitate this opportunity.

On a national basis, integrating design and sales tools increases the sales of custom products and ultimately multiplies the sales of custom products as a percentage of Gross Domestic Product (GDP)[17]. Affluence is produced by greater relevance rather than greater consumption. Societies draw from the elements more sparingly and do more to enhance quality of life with the little they take.

Once again, the sales tools utilized consume virtually no natural resources. Yet the process generates a greater enhancement to the quality of life for all stakeholders than older sales processes ever could. Product customization enhances quality of life. With tools to obtain and record desires and preferences, customization becomes less expensive and less risky for both parties. Facilitating decision making prior to human contact means less sales expense and focused communication.

Happily Ever After

All in all, it has been a very productive day of shopping for Sally. She touched dozens of sites, made several phone calls, picked up one purchase, and set appointments for meetings on custom designs with chosen professionals. But those are activities. Her enhanced quality of life is the

---

[17] Gross Domestic Product represents the monetary value of all goods and service produced by one country in one period, usually one year.

achievement. On the face of it, she has one centerpiece to show for her shopping activity. Inside, she has a great deal more confidence that she can pull off a fantastic Quinceañera celebration for her daughter's 15th Birthday. She has more hope than ever of enjoying a deeper relationship with her in-laws. These things mean more to her than products and services she will acquire. The acquisition of products and services merely facilitate wonderful feelings, much like a great sales process facilitates the acquisition of products and services.

Those merchants who were able to look beyond what they sell to how they could help were best equipped to facilitate Sally's sales process. In 2010, combining this perspective with the energy to proactively provide information and shopping tools often won merchants the first call, over those who passively hoped someone would ask for their sales assistance. In the year 2022, Sally is able to shop among a host of merchants with an understanding of sales integration and the energy to make it work. With greater market transparency, the winning merchant will more often be the one best equipped to meet Sally's needs, which is as it should be. With the cost of software falling in price as quickly as it rises in performance, there is no longer any reason why the smallest of shops can't provide the greatest of service.

As we saw with the curbside pickup, large businesses can perform with caring and understanding. When employees stop feeling like hamsters in a wheel, they do more than just go through the motions. When systems and training emphasize the customer over the policy, employee satisfaction is fueled by intrinsic motivation and customer satisfaction is sure to follow.

Sales remains "people helping people." Sometimes it is a website manager or a software developer. Sometimes it is a delivery person or a phone operator. Sales is not a department, it is how an organization talks with and responds to customers. When an organization is truly customer centric, even the janitor understands how his or her job impacts the organization's ability to facilitate the customer's sales process and enhance quality of life for all involved.

In the year 2022, this kind of thinking and activity is commonplace around the world. Sally and her nearly 8 billion global neighbors will live happily ever after.

Chapter 19

The New Sales Management

We cannot go back to the old days of sending salespeople to knock on doors. It simply is not cost effective and we never seem to call at the right time. The most common paradigm today is listening to the customer through research analysts and trying to build a marketing system that brings shoppers into the physical or online store where the sales process can take place. Sales integration is different. It is about building a sales system that listens and responds wherever the shopper wants to shop.

How can marketing departments take credit for bringing people to the store or site? Did the ads bring in all those people, or was it past sales experiences, delivery, and account management? In my research, I could not find anything that does a convincing job of properly assigning attribution for customer traffic. Nor can I find anything properly assigning attribution for sales. Some auto sales today are no more attributable to the salesperson taking the order than the sale of a hamburger is to the cashier at McDonalds.

Too much time is wasted devising the perfect rewards system. If your employees are not motivated to close deals, you suck as a sales manager, no matter the compensation plan. If some of your employees' need for attribution of the sale is so strong they are insulting other stakeholders whose work touches the customer in the form of listening, matchmaking, demonstrating, closing, delivering, or managing the account, then you have a huge problem. Sales management must become less about managing territories, attribution policies, and commission structures and more about integrated selling processes.

It is time to look at sales management in an entirely new light. The best sales manager may lack in people skills, but excel at thinking through complex processes. This idea will spark controversy for years to come, but the person in power cannot be the person who simply oversees the closing process. Someone needs to think the system through and allocate resources in a way that maximizes revenue and gross profit, rather than just close rates.

Close rates themselves are becoming increasingly meaningless from a macro level. What is the denominator of the close ratio? Is it the number of people who come to the store or the number who thought about coming? Is it the number of people who came to a website where our product can be put into a shopping cart, or the number actually in the shopping cart, or is it the number of people who encountered and considered our product in their shopping process, even if they did so on a site with no shopping cart? Close ratios remain appropriate for individual activities, but not for the larger function of sales spanning a wide range of touchpoints.

The chart below shows the expansion of touchpoints across each phase of sales and marketing. Crossing this with current roles and responsibilities is likely to show many individuals involved in sales (listening through Account Management) that are not currently viewed as part of the sales function or included in sales planning.

Expansion of Where Marketing and Sales Functions Take Place

	Pre-Internet	Current
Advertise	Radio, TV, Print, Outdoor, Direct Mail	Radio, TV, Print, Outdoor, Direct Mail, Search Engines, Independent Websites (Direct, Contextual and Behavioral)
Listen	Store, Call Center	Store, Call Center, Store Site, Manufacturer Site, Shopping Site, Listing Site, Directory Site, Information Site
Match	Store, Call Center	Store, Call Center, Store Site, Manufacturer Site, Shopping Site, Listing Site, Directory Site, Information Site
Demo	Store, Call Center	Store, Call Center, Store Site, Manufacturer Site, Shopping Site, Listing Site, Directory Site, Information Site
Close	Store, Call Center	Store, Call Center, Store Site, Shopping Site
Deliver	In-Store, Shipping	In-Store, Curbside, Shipping, Online (intangibles only)
Manage Account	Store, Account Management Team	Store, AM Team, PURL, Online Account

Business needs more sales professionalism from all things client facing. Regardless of how the organization is structured, there must be recognition that no one in the organization owns the customer; the customer owns the sales process. Businesses must integrate their customer facing efforts to facilitate the needs of the customer or risk losing share to those that do.

Fighting the Bureaucracy

Bureaucracy tends to breed internal competition. While leading the automotive internet practice at J.D. Power and Associates, I became rather popular within the Chrysler Headquarters in Auburn Hills, MI. I knew there was something missing in some of my key relationships, however. One day, a senior manager, desperate to make director soon, took me into his office. The conversation went something like this, "Dennis, I appreciate all your informative and motivational talk about selling more cars; however, my competition is not Ford or Toyota. My competition is the senior manager down the hall. I need to beat him out of the next promotion opportunity. If you want more business from this company, you need to help me make that happen."

I nearly lost it. Had I been carrying a copy of *Atlas Shrugged* I might have beat him over the head with it. A few years prior to the bankruptcies of Chrysler and GM, these organizations were still a bureaucratic mess trying to sell cars to newly empowered shoppers through a distribution network of thousands of independent stores. I was pretty vocal in those days. I did not care about helping my customers win the J.D. Power award for most useful website; I cared about selling cars, and a more useful website helps do that.

The need to come together for a single cause seems so basic, yet the person who is measured by the quantity of leads produced by the website wants to do whatever it takes to move that number, even at the expense of sales. The person who is supposed to help retailers improve their close rates wants the leads scored to minimize the denominator down to only the leads with extreme likelihood to buy. The fact that some shoppers eager to buy will go ignored due to an imperfect system is of no consequence. In too many companies, individuals have a number to move and they move that number with little or no regard for profitability.

It is like hearing, "The ship is sinking, but I did my job." It's not about you. It's not about your job description. It's about keeping the ship afloat and completing the mission, regardless of what it takes or who does it. Revenue and profitability are the metrics for which everyone associated with sales are attributable.

When the shopper is hopping across a multitude of touchpoints, sales becomes teamwork. Selling today involves some people who never closed a sale in their lives. Many lack the people skills it takes to get invited for lunch, no less talk to customers. But without these people onboard, there will be far fewer opportunities to close.

Many operations departments understand this kind of thinking. Most manufacturing plants are no longer built on a Fredrick Taylor model of breaking the process down to the most basic tasks and filling those slots with people who do not understand the big picture. Manufacturing teams put products together. Construction teams build buildings. Surgical teams perform surgeries. Anything with a multitude of touchpoints requires a team approach, and that includes sales.

Comments from Sales VP's about their department being the only ones who bring in revenue do not help the team. Many sales professionals continue to demand control over what customers should and should not be informed about. Not only is it impossible to hide information from customers, ownership of the customer relationship and attribution for the sale is mythical. The customer controls the sales process, and will likely touch the work of multiple employees from varying corners of the organization.

Identify every contact point in your organization that listens to your customers, online of offline. Identify all of the contact points involved with listening, matchmaking, demonstrating, closing, delivery, and account management. Everyone contributing to one of these touchpoints is involved in sales. It does not matter how you structure your organization; your customers are structuring their own sales process. If you had not already decided to become customer centric, it is no problem; your customers are making up your mind for you. The shoppers you want for customers vote with their wallets and elect themselves king of the sales process.

Vendors need to understand your objective and get on board as well. The website provider for one of my auto dealer clients tried to push me into putting a $500 coupon on the homepage of the website. "You got to do it Dennis. Our research shows this will be the most clicked on thing from the home page. Your conversion from visitors to leads will definitely go up."

I'll bet the conversion metric would go up, but will my dealer's profits? If the dealer has to raise the price $500 dollars in order to offer the coupon, fewer shoppers will come from independent sites showing the inflated price to the dealer's site showing the coupon. If the only people coming from listings sites to the dealer's site are those willing to pay an extra $500 over the market price, why offer the coupon? Business is about profit. You can't cut profits to improve a poor conversion ratio. We only pay attention to conversion metrics because they contribute to profitability. Their importance cannot supersede profitability.

Ecommerce trade magazines are loaded with ideas about promotional creativity. Be sure you know what number you are ultimately trying to influence, and it had better have a dollar sign in front of it.

What is the water cooler talk in your organization? If it is more about competition with other departments for resources, recognition, or policy decisions than about meeting the needs of your customers, then you have a huge problem. A bureaucratic approach to B-to-C sales cannot survive in a world of multichannel shoppers. No manager can hold together competing departments well enough to stand up to a firm embracing sales integration.

Any place the shopper is likely to touch in their shopping process is involved in sales, and everyone in the organization needs to understand that. If IT people are working on the public website or the CRM system, then they need to understand sales integration and they need to buy into it.

Sales meetings should look at all sales shortcomings, regardless of where they fall in the reporting structure. The same sales failures occurring offline can occur online as well:

1. Did not listen to the customer
2. Did not make the right match to meet customer wants and needs
3. Did not sufficiently deliver value demonstration relative to shopper wants and needs
4. Comparison of value relative to competitive offerings was flawed or not properly communicated
5. Did not demonstrate the advantage of buying from us
6. Did not ask for the business
7. Did not listen to or respond to objections
8. Did not deliver in a way that facilitated payment, loyalty, and advocacy
9. Did not manage the account to achieve additional sales

Sales meetings must include those answering the phone calls, chats, and emails; those handling any walk-in store traffic; those responsible for the website; and those who work with manufactures, distributors, and independent sites touching the customer in their shopping process.

Marketing or Sales

Academics and practitioners use the term marketing differently. When academics talk about the subject of marketing, the sales function is under that umbrella. Sadly, many universities do not offer sales classes as a marketing requirement or elective, although advertising is a common offering. Nonetheless, we know sales belongs within the marketing program. In business, different departments must have different functions. Conflicts often erupt between sales and marketing departments over turf issues and objectives. Advertising is clearly within the marketing department, and closing the deal is clearly a sales function, but that leaves a great deal of grey area to fight over. Regardless of how responsibilities are divided up among departments, someone needs to understand the big picture, marketing in the broad academic sense.

This book is clearly aimed at a big-picture perspective, yet it is not a book about distant stars and black holes. The intent is to help businesses enact change to enhance quality of life for all stakeholders. Some guidance on implementation is due.

My research into the dividing line between sales and marketing revealed so many different opinions and definitions it could only be concluded that no universal standards exist. It is possible to address the subject from the customer-centric perspective, however. Advertising can be defined as efforts to engage the shopper, but not interact. Interaction with the shopper is a sales function. From this vantage point, marketing departments often do more than advertising, and some sales functions involve people not in the sales department.

Sales professionals dealing only with the close of the sale are generally called cashiers – not a very glorified position. Most retail salespeople in real estate, autos, marine, power sports, jewelry, appliances, electronics and financial services interact with the shopper in a multitude of sales functions, but do not control all online and offline interactions with the shopper. Most ecommerce professionals are not involved with shopper interaction from every site participated on and usually are not involved in delivery.

There must be a path to integrating all touchpoints interacting with the shopper. Reorganization hardly seems like the likely candidate. Engagement and interactivity may take place at the same point of contact. Who runs the show when shoppers are able to interact with interruption advertising? The transition for engaging the shopper to interacting with them may take place within the ad itself. Additionally, consumers continue to modify their shopping habits. It is unlikely any organizational structure will permanently solve the problem.

A team approach, unifying sales, marketing, and any other stakeholders involved in engaging or interacting with the shopper, seems to be in order. Below is a diagram I created for exactly this purpose, the Mouse Chart.

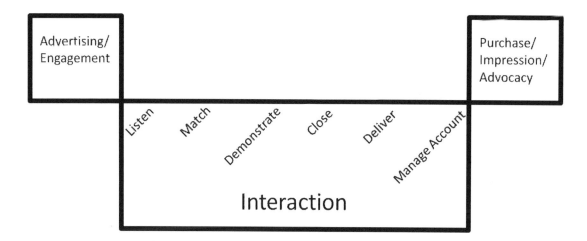

The blank spaces can be annotated with the advertising objectives, sales resource allocations, and the outputs measurements.

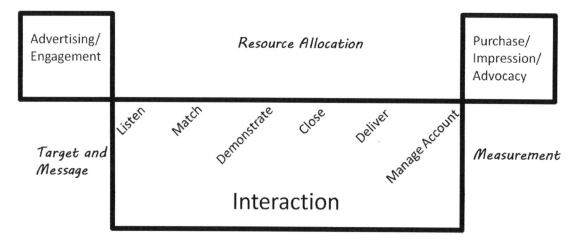

Below is an example of the Mouse Chart used to assist a discussion among decision makers for a fast food chain. Most of the store's resources are allocated to delivery. A clean store, restrooms, and even the parking lot are essential to repurchase. Because most of the chain's revenue comes from repeat customers, the food must be hot and quick. Closing the deal is almost a given. Most of the sales effort at the store is aimed at bringing the customer back. Listening and matchmaking are akin to order taking, but demonstration is different. The stores sell more and receive higher satisfaction scores and more advocacy when pictures of the food, particularly new items, are displayed within the store.

Fast Food

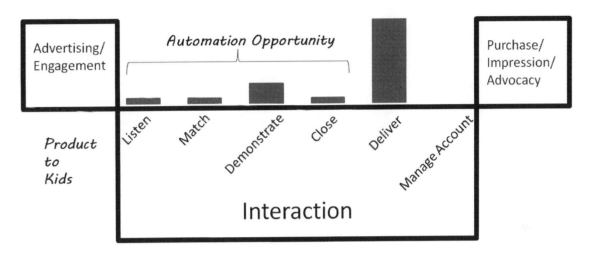

There is talk about extending to late-night hours. To date, the advertising has been limited to showing the product, including free toys, to children. Marketing is reluctant to shift gears and talk about the extended hours with precious dollars designated for mass advertising. They feel the message should come to customers via store signage.

Using the Mouse Chart, everyone quickly realizes the in-store signage conflict and the discussion begins to take shape. Regardless of the outcome, marketing will not be jamming signs up the nose of operations, and stores will not be refusing to post the signs if the decision is made to do so. The chart allows everyone concerned to see the big picture and move forward together.

The next example involves an auto dealership. From experience, they perform best when resources are balanced across all sales functions. The marketing director is interested in the Ai-Dealer tool that will better demonstrate their vehicles online and add a shopping cart allowing sales to be closed online. Most shoppers start their shopping process online and finish the demonstration and close within the store. Yet there are some shoppers who want to close the sale online. There are also customers who come into the store with a vehicle in mind and buy something different. The online portion of the sales process is not perfect and sometimes needs to start over within the store.

Auto Dealer

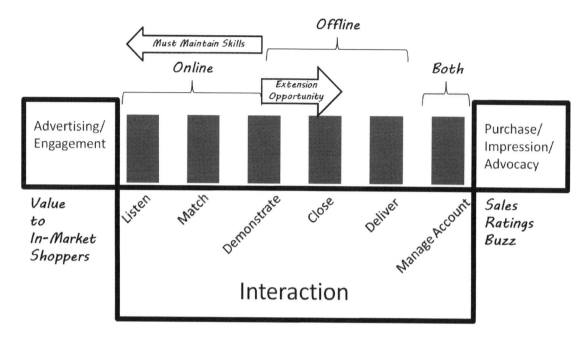

The new product will not replace the need for a well-trained sales team. Those involved in the decision making recognize the online extension cannot come at the expense of sales training for those in the store. It will need to be an additional expense justified by incremental sales and cost reductions. Once the team decides the additional investment is justified without corresponding cuts to training, it is free to move forward with buy-in from all parties.

The next example is a retail bank looking at the deposits side of its business. Most of the profit comes from lending, but most of the loans are made to depositors. The bank targets shoppers who are dissatisfied with their current bank. They frequently blanket communities where a competing bank is going through a change of ownership, change in policy, or experiencing some other event that might generate unsatisfied customers. Their "No Fees" message seems to hit a chord with most of the target audience, however, the bank seems to be churning customers as quickly as it brings them in.

Retail Bank Deposits

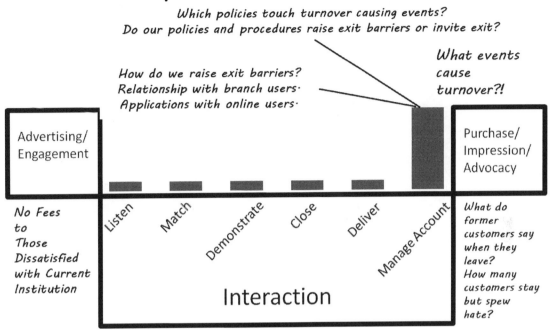

Which policies touch turnover causing events?
Do our policies and procedures raise exit barriers or invite exit?

What events cause turnover?!

How do we raise exit barriers?
Relationship with branch users·
Applications with online users·

Advertising/ Engagement

Purchase/ Impression/ Advocacy

No Fees to Those Dissatisfied with Current Institution

Listen   Match   Demonstrate   Close   Deliver   Manage Account

What do former customers say when they leave? How many customers stay but spew hate?

Interaction

Most of the bank's resources online and within the branch are allocated to helping existing customers. The close rates for new accounts in the bank and online are high, so there is no disagreement about allocation, but should the bank change its advertising focus from acquisition to retention? After some discussion, it becomes clear they have no idea why the bank is losing business. The recognition is made that if the bank is going to aggressively acquire swing users (customers most prone to switching), then it needs to become expert at retaining customers. The first effort will involve rapid research, rather than knee-jerk changes in operations or advertising.

The new sales management cuts across departmental boundaries. Tools like the Mouse Chart will help focus discussions, hasten consensus building, and minimize direction reversals. No tool can make up for a lack of agreement regarding objectives, however. Individuals may continue to have some degree of individual responsibility for individual performance, although, few sales today can truly be attributed to a single person handling all touchpoints related to sales. How each organization finds its own optimal structure and methods of compensation will vary. Every organization must recognize the growing superiority of their consumers in the sales process and the need to integrate across all sales touchpoints.

Even the one-person shop quickly realizes its dependence upon independent websites, vendors, shipping companies, and partnering organizations. Sales is forevermore a team pursuit. Those who embrace this concept will better maximize quality of life for all stakeholders. The salesperson is neither dead nor diminished, but we must look across every interaction with the consumer – human or not – and collectively raise our glasses to a new wave of sales professionalism.

Acknowledgements

Many thanks to Michelle Heinz and Travis Galbraith for their editing help and advice. Thanks to Jennifer Renno for her design work and Mark Dubis for his guidance.

Thanks to my many friends and family for their feedback over the past five years.

Thanks to my loving wife for all her support and encouragement.

Index